VOICES IN THE LABYRINTH
Nature, Man and Science

The Tree of Life

The Tree of Life

Board of Editors

The Tree of Life

Planned and Edited by RUTH NANDA ANSHEN

VOICES IN THE LABYRINTH ≠6

Nature, Man and Science

[Erwin Chargaff]

A CONTINUUM BOOK

THE SEABURY PRESS · NEW YORK

1977
The Seabury Press
815 Second Avenue
New York, New York 10017

Printed in the United States of America

Library of Congress Cataloging in Publication Data

Chargaff, Erwin.   Voices in the labyrinth.
(The Tree of life ; 3) (A Continuum book)
Includes bibliographical references.
1. Science—Social aspects.   2. Science—Philosophy.
3. Research.   I. Title.   II. Series.
Q175.5.C49   301.24'3   77-8301   ISBN 0-8164-9322-7

Contents

The Tree of Life

"Hope deferred maketh the
heart sick,
But when desire cometh, it is a
Tree of Life."
Book of Proverbs 13:12

Inevitably, towards the end of an historical period, when thought and custom have petrified into rigidity, and when the elaborate machinery of civilization opposes and represses man's more noble qualities, life stirs again beneath the hard surfaces. Nevertheless, this attempt to define the purpose of *The Tree of Life* series is set forth with profound trepidation. Man is living through a period of extreme darkness. There is moral atrophy, an internal destructive radiation within us as the result of the collapse of values hitherto cherished—but now betrayed. We seem to be face to face with an apocalyptic destiny. The anomie, the chaos, surrounding us is causing almost a lethal disintegration of the person as well as ecological and demographic disaster. Our situation is indeed desperate. And there is no glossing over the deeper and unresolved tragedy with which our lives are filled. Science itself as now practised tells us what *is*, but not what *ought* to be; *de*scribing but not *pre*scribing.

And yet, we cannot say "yes" to our human predicament. The Promethean protest must not be silenced by lame submission. We have been thrown into this indifferent universe, and although we cannot change its structure, we can temporarily, for our own lifetime and for the life of the human race, build shelters of meaning, of empathy and compassion. Thus, for the fleeting moment that our lives fill, we can rise above time and indifferent eternity, struggling for the ray of light that pierces through this darkness. We can transcend the indifference of nature or, to be blasphemous, this badly messed up creation, and listen to the "still, small voice"—the source of hope without which there would be no humanity at all. For in this way, we can again reaffirm the glory of the human spirit.

This series is dedicated to that kind of understanding which may be compared with the way birds understand the singing of other birds. We, as men, women and children, need to learn to understand and respect each other, beyond exploitation, beyond self-interest, and to experience what it means *to be* by discovering, if we can, the secret of life.

My introduction to *The Tree of Life* is not, of course, to be construed as a prefatory essay to each individual volume. These few pages simply endeavor to set forth the general aim and purpose of this series as a whole. This statement hopefully may serve the reader with a new orientation in his thinking, more specifically defined by those scholars who have been invited to participate in this intellectual, spiritual and moral endeavor so desperately needed in our time, and who recognize the relevance of that non-discursive experience of life which the discursive, analytical, method alone is unable to convey.

The Tree of Life has summoned the world's most concerned thinkers to rediscover the experience of *feeling* as well as of thought. Such is the difference between the Tree of Life and the Tree of Knowledge. The Tree of Life presides over the coming of the possible fulfillment of self-awareness—not the isolated, alienated self, but rather the participation in the life-process with other lives and other forms of life. It is a cosmic force and may possess liberating powers of allowing man to become what he is.

The further aim of this series is certainly not, nor could it be, to disparage knowledge or science. The authors themselves in this effort are adequate witness to this fact. Actually, in viewing the role of science, one arrives at a much more modest judgment of the role which it plays in our

whole body of knowledge. Original knowledge was probably not acquired by us in the active sense; most of it must
have been given to us in the same mysterious way as, and
perhaps as part of, our consciousness. As to content and
usefulness, scientific knowledge is an infinitesimal fraction
of natural knowledge. However, it is a knowledge, the
structure of which is endowed with beauty because its abstractions satisfy our urge for specific knowledge much
more fully than does natural knowledge itself, and we are
justly proud of it because we can call it our own creation. It
teaches us clear thinking and the extent to which clear
thinking helps us to order our sensations it is a marvel
which fills the mind with ever new and increasing admiration and awe. But science must now begin to include the
realm of human values, lest even the memory of what it
means to be human be forgotten.

It is also the aim of *The Tree of Life* to present solid analyses of the critical issues of our time which, though rest-
ing on an intuitively conceived basis, are scholarly produc-
tions in the true sense of the word. And although there is
a concern with the non-discursive element of all knowledge, the fruits the scholars in this Series hope to gather
will be an expansion of such knowledge, open to verification and experience. For we are living in an emergency situation which requires approaches with practical consequences. And these consequences are not confined to the
realm of political action; they refer as much to a reformation
of science and education as to a renewal of ethics and
human attitudes and behavior.

The gap between religion and science has been largely
eliminated by modern advances in our concepts of cosmology, the nature of matter, the forces that move the universe and created life and the nature of mind and the
mind-brain relation. Therefore science indeed, if not misused, becomes extremely relevant and must admit into its
orbit revelation, faith and intuition.

A new dimension has now in the latter half of this twen-
tieth century appeared in our consciousness in spite of the
tyranny of our technocratic society. We yearn to *experience*

that kind of intuition of a reality which allows us to remember that we are *human*. And this consciousness of what it means to be human is an all-pervading command which our nature summons us to respect everywhere: in science, in philosophy, commerce, revolution, religion, art, sanctity and even in error which needs to be transformed, when the heart and mind of humankind attain a certain depth of mastery in the power of discovering new horizons and taking great risks.

Self-awareness is an incomparable spiritual gain since it begets *life* unencumbered by excessive intellectual baggage. The Tree of Knowledge, important and fruitful in itself, is no substitute for the Tree of Life, the fruits of which Adam and Eve did not eat in the primordial garden. Now we are, so to speak, given a second chance since the Tree of Life and the Tree of Knowledge have one and the same root. Self-awareness then becomes actual. The question is, however, how the conditions may be provided. This is a matter of the interplay of freedom and destiny.

The question pursued in the many respective disciplines expressed through the invited scholars, is how the actualization of the *experience of life*, not merely the idea about life, may be achieved through the fulfillment of the potentialities in each one of us. In order to answer this question, we must consider, as this series tries to do, the dynamics of life, and the historical dimensions in an anticipatory way so that the goal always remains in the path. This last and all-embracing dimension of life comes to its full realization in man as an aspect of the universe and of matter itself. Man is the bearer of the spirit when the conditions for its realization are present.

We bow to the *life force*, to that mysterious energy which creates life. The observation of a particular potentiality of being, whether it is that of another species or of a person, actualizing themselves in time and space, has led to the concept of *life*, life as the actuality of being. A tension is always present between matter and form in all existence. If the actualization of the potential is a structural condition of all beings, and if this actualization is called "life," then the universal concept of life, in all its manifold expressions among all species and not only in mankind, becomes unavoidable. Thus *The Tree of Life* endeavors to define the *multidimensionality of all life*, the inorganic with its mystery as well as the organic with its mastery, the psychological, historical and the spiritual. Such is the "alchemy" of life. Such is the immediate experience of the *consciousness* of life, of *living life itself*. Such is the new threshold on which we stand.

Newton would have despaired if he could have envisaged the duality of the universe to which his work was to lead, and to the determinism which so completely eroded the Aristotelian view of purpose. It seems to be our good fortune that the recent discoveries in science have themselves, in turn, undermined the possibility of belief in a universe contingent only on those aspects of nature which can be revealed by science alone. Could it be that the world is approaching a remarkable synthesis of the disparate issues in science and religion which have been such an obstacle in this generation?

Emphasis in Western culture has been placed, for the greater part, on knowledge which too often has degenerated into quantitative information. The fact that probability and certainty, faith and knowledge, require intuition has frequently been ignored while the data of observation, requiring only the act of observing with one's physical eyes, exclusive of the creative process of intuition, of envisaging, have been extolled as primary in human consciousness, and have been accepted as more important than the experience of life itself.

Anthropocentric values superimposed on all life—whether organic or inorganic—are evidences of a form of power incompatible with the reality of the multidimensionality of living creatures in whatever animal, entomological, even perhaps cosmological and human forms *life* may manifest itself. There is no justification for enforcing the concept of causality on the entire universe as the only possible form of relationship. In particular, while many phenomena exhibited by living beings can be foreseen on the basis of causal relations with the past, we should be aware of the possibility of relations of another type, for example, the circularity of reason and consequences in addition to the linearity of cause and effect.

There is abundant anthropological evidence that supports the intuitive perspective of the experience of life and life processes and indicates that our implicit knowledge of phenomena may be as old as humanity itself. And we can now begin to use this knowledge as a regular part of our scientific understanding of consciousness.

The Tree of Life, a series of volumes on a variety of vital problems and written by the most concerned thinkers of our time, attempts to show the structural kinship of life and knowledge and to overcome the false dualism which indeed has never existed, since unity and reality are one.

We are faced with planning and with choice. We can change the course of human life. What do we want to do with this newly achieved power? What is to become of the freedom of the individual in a genetically, politically, and socially engineered society? The implications of genetic engineering are especially serious and we have now reached the time when we must ask ourselves: Even though some things are possible, are they desirable? The centers of economic and even political power become less and less national, and the state and its corporations are powers, not institutions serving the people. The spirit has petrified in the lava of phenomena.

We cannot know where our new knowledge of life will lead us. Our fate, as the fate of the world, or the cosmos, is not fixed. All this depends on chance, freedom, will, and purpose. Life itself is a struggle against randomness. It strives to replace randomness by arrangements which give some aesthetic satisfaction and which may have some meaning. And even if we, as humanity, in coming generations of greater longevity, do indeed endure, it will require a wealth of further complexity and organization. Perhaps the earth itself—and even some galaxies—and mankind as well, will some day disappear, by accident, inability of adaptation and mutation, or the universe's power of depleting itself. Yet our consciousness and the values locked up in it are now entrusted to us, waiting for our decision for a life lived, not as a fragment of knowledge or information alone, but as an active element of experience.

Turning our backs for a moment on the vast cosmic challenges which confront man in his perceptions of the cosmology of life, and looking into ourselves for an elementary analysis and understanding of our intuitive conception of past and present, we find it to be essentially based on two facts. First, our need to accept at all times a single, unitary structure forever present in spite of its complexity. For in any sequence of states of consciousness we may live through, each is simultaneous with the whole in all its parts. Second, the fact of memory, by which we can embrace in our present consciousness elements of a previous state of being (what Plato called *anamnesis,* or spiritual recollection of other lives lived in each of us before our present life). Thus we recognize, if only at times dimly or subconsciously, that there is the same simultaneity in unbroken continuity of past, present, and future and manifesting itself as fresh, current happenings. We compare these vestiges of the past with the facts of the present and derive therefrom our notion of the passage of time.

Confronted by the difficulties of finding a physical interpretation of the temporal characteristics of consciousness, we may assume one or another of two distinct attitudes. The first, which should be called defeatist, is to divide once and for all the universe into two separate parts: the world of mind and the world of matter. This means of course completely abandoning the effort to grasp and understand the whole, or life itself. The other attitude is to use any new notions—such as those derived recently from microphysics, psychology, and biology—in an effort to move toward the basic unity of matter and mind, to reconcile the present unity of consciousness not only with the chain of causation but with the mystery of life itself. The erroneous "gap" between matter and mind has been artificially postulated by man in order to facilitate the analysis of their parts.

It is suggested that the mystical Tree of Life is at the

same time the tree of transcendent authority—as distinct from mere power. Each branch of this tree has a common root at times unknown and even unknowable in a logical sense. It can be intuited and experienced since it is not only the root of all roots, it is also the sap of the Tree. Every branch represents an attribute and exists by virtue of the hidden transcendent authority inherent in it. And this Tree of Life is the substance of the universe. It grows throughout the whole of creation and spreads its branches through all its ramifications. Thus, all mundane and created things exist only because something of the authority of the Tree of Life lives and acts through them. The body and the soul, though different in nature—one being material, the other spiritual—nevertheless constitute an organic whole and are *substantially* the same. The conception of life as an organism has the advantage of answering the question why there are different manifestations of the transcendent quality of life itself. For is not the organic life of the spirit one and the same, although, for example, the function of the hands differs from that of the eyes? The universe is in man as man is in the universe.

We have forgotten that throughout antiquity, down to the advent of the experimental sciences, every movement or change in the outside world had a direct bearing on man. Since human affairs were linked by an interlocking system of correspondence—with the planets, the animal world, the four elements—nothing that occurred in the macrocosm but that it had some impact upon them. This tangled network of interrelationships and concordances collapsed by virtue of the discoveries of mechanics in the universe by Copernicus, Galileo, Newton, and Einstein; only the movement of objects and the laws that govern them were considered important and relevant to reality. Man himself was forgotten. Whether these laws of mechanics concern planets or molecules, these movements and laws were considered no longer directly related to the complicated events that together make up the major portion of our daily lives.

Hand in hand with this dehumanization of man and the world, a profound transformation of its laws took place, giving birth to a new conception of causality. The universe assumed a continuous geometrical structure in which there was no place for individual beings, human or animal. While this kind of revolutionary view of reality managed for a long time to satisfy the demands of experimental science, it administered a profound shock to all of us who remained attached to the basic truth, the beliefs and hypotheses which are in themselves totalities.

The scientific world, as we have inherited it, with all its plethora of information, its technology, does not present a picture of the real world and of man in it. It gives us an abundance of factual information, puts all our data in a magnificently consistent order, but it remains ominously silent about all that is really near to our hearts, all that really matters to a lived life. It cannot tell us anything about red and blue, bitter and sweet, physical pain and physical delight; it knows nothing of what is beautiful and ugly, good and evil, joy and sorrow, the infinite and the finite. Within the scientific world-picture, all these experiences take care of themselves; they are amply accounted for by direct, energetic interplay. Even the human body's movements are its own. The scientific-technological interpretation of man and the world allows us to imagine the total display as that of a mechanical clockwork which ticks away without there being any consciousness, will, freedom, justice, memory, tragedy, endeavor, pain, delight, tears, laughter, sacrifice, moral responsibility, aesthetic experience or religious insight. Man has been relegated, he is expendable, evaporated in this scientific-technological world-structure.

The philosopher, seeking the essence of life, is confronted with the desperate drive to discover some basis, some anti-mechanism, since his entire experience of vital feelings and function, his intrinsic values, warn him against a deterministic and mechanical image which is spurious. For our problem seems to be therefore that every scientist is constantly faced with the objective description of data by which we understand communication in unambiguous terms. But how can objectivity of description be retained during the growth of experience within and beyond daily life occurrences? The widening of the conceptual framework has not only served to restore order within the respective branches of knowledge, but has also disclosed analogies in the analysis and synthesis of *experience* in apparently separated domains of knowledge, suggesting the possibility of an ever more embracing insight into the nature of life itself. Yet, life is not isomorphic with knowledge. Life draws us far beyond knowledge and happily transcends it. And when this truth is realized, then the system of scientific knowledge may be made the vehicle for the actualization of new emotions. The fact of consciousness as applied to ourselves as well as to others is indispensable when dealing with the human situation. In view of this, one may well wonder how materialism and determinism—the doctrine that life could be explained by sophisticated combinations of physical and chemical laws—could have for so long been accepted by the majority of scientists. Obviously there is something in nature, in the nature of man, that transcends matter. For now nature, it is suggested, may be on the point of being disenthralled from the deterministic demon; and although the assertion of determinism is certainly possible, it is by no means necessary, and when examined closely, is not even practicable.

Therefore, the authors in *The Tree of Life* summon us to ask the question: What does it mean to be human? Why do we feel, as we indeed do, at least some of us, that there is no break in the laws of continuity applicable to the universe as to man? For the present is filled with the past and pregnant with the future. And we now must realize that the finite is akin to the infinite, as man is akin to eternity, and that this kinship allows him like the transcendent demiurge to fashion the world, and that the performance of this task is the truly human obligation. This constitutes the present profound change in man's consciousness. The fruit he has eaten from the Tree of Life has carved out for him a difficult but rewarding path: a revolt against traditionally accepted scientific principles and a yearning for that qualitative metamorphosis in which the new stage of consciousness comes into existence as the result of a decisive jolt and is characteristic of a life of the spirit which, when coupled with the organic development, is like the planting of a seed whose successive unfolding has given man the nourishing fruit of the Tree of Life, for man's organism is instinct with the drive toward primal unity.

Man is capable of making the world what it is destined to be: a community of people who have the resources of each particular region in common and who share in the goods and cultures and knowledge, a task far from being completed. We are faced with a serious problem, since the wavelength of change is shorter than the lifespan of man and the time required for adaptation and mutation is limited. Life itself is threatened. Not only must we continue to emphasize the pressing problems and immediate needs, not only as a goal but as a solution, to recognize the indissoluble union between progress and that of liberty, virtue, and respect for the natural rights of man, but also the effects of life on the destruction of prejudice.

The volumes in *The Tree of Life* endeavor to emphasize the pulse of the present and its meaning for the future. The past is with us. The present summons us. Our sociological theories, our political economy, our scientific potentialities and achievements, our religious and metaphysical principles and our doctrines of education are derived from an unbroken tradition of great thinkers and of practical examples from the age of Plato in the fifth century B.C. to the end of the last century. The whole tradition is warped by the vicious assumption that each generation should substantially live amid the conditions governing the lives of its fathers and should transmit those conditions to mold with equal force the lives of their children. *We are now living in the first period of human history for which this assumption is false.*

Other subjects to be explored by the invited authors are problems of communications media which must awaken to their responsibility and to be conducted by men and women who bring not only method but substance; in other words, *live* explorations into all problems of contemporary society in the East and the West, and who will not be automatic, static products of an established social culture. It is the permanent "energy" of that which is essentially *man* which must be transmitted from one generation to another, thereby giving criteria to judgments and actions so that the continuity of human life and the evolutionary force which is *mind* may be preserved. Thus we maintain an openness to the coexistence of all qualities that characterizes the living world.

No individual destiny can be separated from the destiny of the universe. Whitehead has stated the doctrine that every event, every step or process in the universe involves both effects from past situations and the anticipation of future potentialities. Basic for this doctrine is the assumption that the course of the universe results from a multiple and never ending complex of steps developing out of one another. Thus in spite of all evidence to the contrary, we conclude that there is a continuing and permanent energy of that which is not only man but all of life itself. And it is for this reason that we espouse life. For not an atom stirs in matter, organic and inorganic, that does not have its cunning duplicate in Mind. And faith in *life* creates its own verification.

Ruth Nanda Anshen
New York

I am indebted and grateful to Professor Chiang Yee for calling my attention to the Chinese ideograph, meaning *LIFE* (the fourth century B.C.) which is used on the jacket and binding of the volumes in *The Tree of Life* as its colophon.

R.N.A.

Preface

T his book is not in the first place addressed to professional scientists, though those who like to think while they run may enjoy, and even profit from, reading it. It is directed to people who take a serious interest in the position of the sciences in our time. This position is no longer what it was in the post-Victorian glow of settled and unquestioned security. Enormous world wars, unprecedented devastations, heart-rending dislocations have changed more than the face of this earth; and values, long established and taken for granted, are being challenged, though nothing much can be put in their place.

The recent past has witnessed many expressions of a strong revulsion from science, often combined with a dislike of technocracy. There are those who consider science as the cause of all evils of our time; for others it is merely one of the symptoms. I belong to neither group. I do believe, however, that, as every human activity engaging the mind and the heart of man, science—its foundations and its effects—deserves to be taken seriously. This I have tried to do, though not without the weapons of humor, irony, and even satire.

It is, of course, silly to mount an attack on science as such, rather than on the uses to which science has been put by a depraved time; for science as a response to the urge to search for truth, even if only partial truth, about nature is presumably as old as humanity. It is, on the other hand, imperative to criticize the excesses to which the sciences and, especially, their practitioners, the scientists, so often are being driven by our greedy and publicity-drunk age.

Science is so immense an undertaking of humanity, there are so many disparate disciplines claiming to be scientific, with codes of conduct reaching from the sublime to the ridiculous, that even a scientist who has explored one branch of the enormous tree for an entire lifetime cannot but speak as a layman. This is not without advantage: the position of the critic as an "outsider on the inside," as I have once called myself, may afford a view of the whole that will avoid the hollow ponderousness with which such problems are often discussed.

The name of the series in which this volume appears calls up mythical memories of the history of the world. Of the many trees "eastward in Eden" two are mentioned in the Bible: the Tree of Life "in the midst of the garden" and the Tree of Knowledge of good and evil. When I decided, many years ago, to enter science it was in the belief that the two trees were the same. After some time I realized that this was far from being the case. Both trees bear fruit. Twelve fruits, one for each month, does the Tree of Life, *lignum vitae,* bear in the Apocalypse (22:2). The fruits of the other tree are less recommended (Genesis 2:17); but it is with them that our century has been gorged. To mention one example about which this volume has something to say, our present understanding of the mechanisms of heredity—or better, the use we are getting ready to make of this knowledge—represents the culmination of all attempts by the natural sciences to invade the sacred precincts of life.

I still believe that science need not be the evil force that it has become in our time; that, in fact, an entirely different form of science is imaginable; that it—"the other science"— did exist, and found its expression, in several great scientists of the past. Although I still believe all this, I cannot see where the regenerative forces can arise. The hope that all this cannot go on much longer is joined to the fear that it will.

For the section that gave the title to this book, I have chosen the dialogue form which permits a free and widely ranging discussion of concepts and ideas that find no ready place in more conventional works. The three dialogues and the short epilogue presented here proceed gradually from the particular to the general. Although they are in no way reproductions of actual conversations, many of the more inane remarks were, at one time or another, contributed by friends or colleagues.

The first dialogue was written in 1961 and published, in a slightly different form, as the last chapter of a book: *Essays on Nucleic Acids* (Elsevier, Amsterdam, 1963). The other dialogues were written in 1972 and 1973. The fabled beasts forming the titles may require some explanation. For *Amphisbaena* I quote *Webster's Third New International Dictionary:* "A serpent in classical mythology having a head at one end and being capable of moving in either direction." As regards *Ouroboros*, I must go to more recondite sources. The serpent devouring its own tail, forming a circle around the words *hen to pan* (One Is All), is depicted in one of the earliest alchemical writings extant, one of the magical papyri of Leiden, around 250 A.D. It was a symbol of eternity, and Jean Paul calls it "the serpent of eternity." *Chimaera* is more of a hybrid—a monster with a lion's head, a goat's body and a serpent's tail.

Erwin Chargaff

1. The Paradox of Biochemistry

The paradox of my title is stated easily: biochemistry, by its very name, is the chemistry of life. But, as so often in the sciences, there prevails a peculiar uncertainty principle: the biochemist must kill the cell before he can study what it contains. Before turning to the problems of biochemistry, however, I shall first sketch an even greater paradox, namely, the paradox of science. Science, in my way of using the word, stands for the natural sciences, *i.e.*, those branches of human knowledge and the search for knowledge that concern themselves with the innumerable aspects of matter, the structure of materials, their conversions or reactions, and the laws governing them.

Science then is the search for truth about nature, and as such it is an eminently intellectual undertaking of humanity, or—it would perhaps be safer to say—of the Western mind. In saying that, I may have said too much; some would maintain that science is a search not for the true but for the plausible. But society has never been particularly anxious to tolerate a search for truth, and even less to pay for it. And it makes relatively little difference whether you think in this connection of Socrates and the hemlock, Galilei and the Inquisition, or the more recent victims of the various witch-hunting committees of the "Great Democracies." Somehow, and deep down darkly, the act of searching and learning has always been considered a revolutionary act. When I hear the many silly jokes about the Chinese with their little red book, my emphasis is neither on "little" nor on "red"—it is on "book."

There is another point. Like all things of the mind, science is a brittle thing: it becomes absurd when you look at it too closely. It is designed for few at a time, not as a mass profession. But now we have megascience: an immense apparatus discharging in a minute more bursts of knowledge than humanity is able to assimilate in a lifetime. Each of us has two eyes, two ears and, I hope, one brain. We cannot even listen to two symphonies at the same time. How do we get out of the horrible cacophony that assails our minds day and night? We have to learn, as others did, that if science is a machine to make more science, a machine to grind out so-called facts of nature, not all facts are equally worth knowing. Students, in other words, will have to learn to forget most of what they have learned. This process of forgetting must begin after each exam, but never before. The Ph.D. is essentially a license to start unlearning.

The impact of science on human life has been both very beneficial and very disastrous. If you have a rosy temperament, as I decidedly have not, you will be inclined to emphasize the sweetness of the fruits. I have become sensitized to their astringency, their bitterness. Yet, in a world whose greatest ideal seems to be to buy cheap and to sell dear, the profession of science has remained one of the more decent ones. This affords a measure of consolation, though not for long; for when a country rots, everything rots.

There is no question in my mind that we live in one of the truly bestial centuries in human history. There are plenty of signposts for the future historian, and what do they say? They say "Auschwitz" and "Dresden" and "Hiroshima" and "Vietnam" and "Napalm." For many years we all woke up to the daily body count on the radio. And if there were a way to kill people with the B Minor Mass, the Pentagon-Madison Avenue axis would have found it. Just as the streets of our cities are full of filth and crime, our scientific imagination has become brutalized, torn as it is by equally unattainable ideals, none of which is really worth attaining. The modern version of Buridan's ass has a Ph.D., but no time to grow up as he is undecided between making a Leonardo da Vinci in the test tube or planting a Coca Cola sign on Mars. Because the world is becoming uninhabitable, we reach for the stars; but shall we not succeed in making them equally uninhabitable? No doubt, we are the first generation that could think of building an atomic fire under mankind. We can incinerate them all; but no radioactive phoenix will rise from these ashes. You may suspect that I believe Prometheus got what was coming to him. Did he bring the fire to the world? That was nice. But did he perhaps immediately afterwards proceed to set the whole world afire? Were not the gods right in cutting off his research grants? Greek mythology may, of course, not tell us the entire story. Perhaps, the gods got so embroiled in trying to wipe out a disobedient little people that their National Institute of Cosmogony ran out of money for basic research.

But let us turn to more specific questions and to the place biochemistry occupies in what I hesitate to call the hierarchy of the sciences. The two basic natural sciences, one could say, are physics and chemistry. Physics deals specifically with the fundamental structure of matter, with energy, with motion, etc.; chemistry deals with the transformation of matter, with the detailed description of its composition, etc. One might say—but this is, of course, a crude oversimplification—that physics is concerned with atoms and chemistry with molecules.

There is one important thing that these sciences have in common and that distinguishes them from biology: they are inherently and legitimately statistical sciences, dealing with enormous numbers of identical components. If we have a bar of pure gold—I am speaking of the good old days when the United States still had a bar of gold—or a solution of pure glucose, we can be sure that every gold atom, every glucose molecule, will behave in entirely the same manner. Should we find anomalies, we would not speak of physical variation or of chemical variation; we would call it a contamination. But we have all heard of biological variation. We have only to look at our neighbors to realize how deplorably different various representatives of *Homo sapiens* are. But where does biology, and consequently biochemistry, come in? First, again at the risk of oversimplification, we may posit that the living cell plays the same role in biology that the molecule does in chemistry and the atom in physics. Biochemistry then deals ideally with the chemistry of the living cell and biophysics with its physical characteristics. But is there then a level at which the living cell can be treated purely as a chemical system? Is the living cell as derivable from chemistry as a chemical system is from physics? The majority of biochemists will answer "Yes"; a large, though diminishing, number of biologists will answer "No." I shall answer nothing, reserving to myself that rare prerogative of the free man to say "I don't know."

Still, we may play with a sort of hierarchy as regards the living cell and say that the parameters of biology are something like physics$\rightarrow$chemistry$\rightarrow x \rightarrow y \rightarrow z$. All, therefore, depends on what x, y, and z are and on whether they exist. The most orthodox practitioners of the exact sciences will claim that there is no x, y, and z. They will say that the laws of physics and chemistry are sufficient to explain life—and life is the substance of biology—and that all biological phenomena can be reduced to chemistry and physics. These people, who used to be called antivitalists, are now referred to more elegantly as reductionists. Their writings exude a touching optimism, which can often have funny consequences and may, incidentally, be one of the reasons why, at a time when all the arts have exploded skyhigh, the natural sciences have remained peculiarly Victorian.

Other scientists, especially in the early days, assumed that x, y, and z do exist and they spoke of a vital force which was necessary for the manufacture and functioning of the materials making up the living organism. This branch of natural philosophy was called "vitalism"; now one could speak of "nonreductionism." With the onset of organic chemistry, which showed that many compounds made by the living cell could be synthesized in the laboratory, vitalism began to be discredited, and perhaps rightly so since what is the use of substituting a name for an explanation?

At the same time one must admit that our present-day physics and chemistry cannot furnish us with a full explanation of the functioning of the living cell. The key words here are "biological function." We do not speak of the function of the rock—except as part of an ecological system—in the sense in which we speak of the function of adenosine triphosphate. There is a transcendence in biology that is essentially foreign to chemistry or physics. The chemist presides over a comfortably closed universe, that of the biologist is wide open. Chemists do not have to bother about what could be called the sociology of molecules; but the cell practices a form of togetherness for which the New York subway in the rush hour is a most inadequate model. The cell is certainly more than a chemical slum. What is the "more"? This is another way of saying that our present knowledge does not supply us with a sufficient explanation of the organization of the living cell.

It is, of course, conceivable that when we have learned more than we know now a more complete reduction will become possible. In other words, there is still plenty of scope for the year 2069 and even 2169. But can we really believe that, if we keep on plodding for another 200 years or so, suddenly submicroscopic angels will be seen carrying a sign, "Now you know all about nature"? Actually, knowledge of nature is an expanding universe, continually creating ever greater circumferences of ignorance, a concept that can be expressed in the words, "the more we know, the less we know."

For many centuries biology, the science of life, remained entirely descriptive. Only in the eighteenth century did it become codifying when naturalists such as Linné and Buffon attempted to bring some order into the baffling multiplicity of living species. In the nineteenth century biology became dynamic, when the concept of the cell as the basic unit of living systems was formulated by Schleiden and

Schwann and later by Virchow. From then on it did not take long for the realization that life is based on the maintenance, the propagation or, in the case of viruses, the exploitation of the cell. There is a famous saying of Virchow about the continuity of life stating that every cell must come from a cell. But how about the first cell, how was it formed? Since the time when the principles of evolution became popularized this question has been asked repeatedly, and many studies on the "origin of life" have been undertaken. To what extent these studies belong to biochemistry and whether they are not one of the more elegant forms of science fiction remains undecided. If I were given a choice between the Book of Genesis and the latest text on the origin of life I might conclude that Moses was by far the better writer.

We are agreed then that biochemistry is the chemistry of the living cell. But do we know what life is? In *Webster's Unabridged Dictionary* I find a most inept definition—"Life, the quality that distinguishes a vital and functional being from a dead body or purely chemical matter"—illustrated by a silly quotation from Mary Shelley: "my ability to give life to an animal." I wonder whether Mary Shelley ever tried.

Our ignorance of what life is will, of course, not keep us from continuing to be biochemists, but it may introduce a measure of humility. Moreover, I hope you will realize that there are many types of chemical studies that can be performed on the living organism. The intermediary metabolism of living cells can, for instance, be studied with great precision, especially since the discovery of isotopic tracers made available an enormous number of labeled compounds. In addition, a large part of biochemistry is devoted to *in vitro* studies with isolated and purified systems.

But does all this really bring us much nearer to the core problem, the chemistry of life? How many of the questions can we answer that paleolithic man could have asked? The mumbling priesthood of ancient Egypt may have been replaced by the lobbying scientists of Washington; they are more numerous, but hardly much wiser. We still cannot describe to you the chemistry of the living cell, though we have a pretty good idea of the dead one.

We know that a cell may contain innumerable substances, but that its bulk will be made up of four principal groups: proteins, nucleic acids, polysaccharides, and lipids. There is, of course, no hierarchy in the cell; all components are equally essential, though accidents and nutritional variations may have some influence, especially on the relative quantities. The cell contains an enormous variety of proteins. All the catalytic functions of the cell—the making and breaking of cellular constituents—are performed by specialized proteins, the enzymes.

The essential functions of the nucleic acids have been recognized only in the last twenty years. DNA (deoxyribonucleic acid) is generally thought to specify the hereditary properties of the cell: we are told that in it there are encoded all those characteristics of the cell that can be transmitted throughout the generations. Whether this essentially Manichaean picture of an inexorable demiurgos exacting retribution from the offspring for errors of which the ancestors had been innocent—whether this view of living nature, based, after all, on observations of very simple living systems studied under controlled conditions, should be extended to the incredible multiformity, to this glorious and miserable disorder of the entire realm of life, remains to be seen. The concatenations of fate and accident to which human beings are subject during and even before their lives are too complex to yield to so simpleminded a grammar.

In any event, there exists considerable evidence that DNA represents the sum of the genetic determinants and that it is under its direction that the various ribonucleic acids (RNA) are produced, by a process often described as "transcription." The various RNA species can, in turn, be shown to be concerned with the synthesis of the many proteins of the cell.

About the rest we know little. And this rest is very large: polysaccharides, lipids, membranes and cell walls, etc. But even if we knew all about all cellular constituents, where would this lead us? We should still be faced by the horrendous problem of the peaceful coexistence in the living cell of all these huge molecules—many of them, in the test tube, lethal to each other.

Sometimes during sleepless nights I wonder whether a time that had not grown rich and fat and dull on giant computerized corporations would also have viewed the cell as a society of slaves, all carrying Social Security numbers. Each period has the vision of nature that it deserves.

Science deals with data, with what is given—it does not ask about the giver; it collects facts, what is made—but it does not inquire about the maker. Science is wonderfully equipped to answer the question "How?" But it gets terribly confused when you ask it the question "Why?" It is this givenness of nature that has, in fact, constituted the main strength of the natural sciences: their freedom to go ever deeper into what is here. Our modern sciences began, one could say, around the beginning of the seventeenth century. Until that time humanity had been nestling in the hollow of the hand of God. They knew the "How?" because they knew the "Why?" But then the question "How really?" began to be asked ever more urgently, and this went on for 300 years. Now the light of knowledge—ever bigger and more fragmented—has become so strong that the world threatens to fade before it. We are able not only to register facts of nature, but also to create new ones. We manipulate nature as if we were stuffing an Alsatian goose. We create new forms of energy; we make new elements; we kill the crops; we wash the brains. I can hear them in the dark sharpening their lasers. Soon the hereditary determinants themselves will begin to be manipulated. I am afraid the "dark satanic mills" of which Blake wrote will be no less satanic for being brightly illuminated.

2. A Quick Climb Up
Mount Olympus

Unfortunately, I hear it often said of a scientist, "He's got charisma." What is meant by "charisma" is not easy to say. It seems to refer to some sort of ambrosial body odor: an emanation that can be recognized most easily by the fact that "charismatic" individuals expect to be paid at least two-ninths more than the rest, unless Schweitzer or Einstein chairs are available. But what does one do if two men share one charisma?

This would certainly seem to be the case with the two who popularized base-pairing in DNA and conceived the celebrated structural model that has become the emblem of a new science, molecular biology. This model furnishes the title of this "personal account," and Watson describes it, without undue modesty, as "perhaps the most famous event in biology since Darwin's book." Whether Gregor Mendel's ghost concurred in this rodomontade is not stated. The book as a whole testifies, however, to a regrettable degree of strand separation which one would not have thought possible between heavenly twins; for what is Castor without Pollux?

This is the beginning of Chapter One of Watson's book[1]:

I have never seen Francis Crick in a modest mood. Perhaps in other company he is that way, but I have

9

never had reason so to judge him. It has nothing to do with his present fame. Already he is much talked about, usually with reverence, and someday he may be considered in the category of Rutherford or Bohr. But this was not true when, in the fall of 1951, I came to the Cavendish Laboratory of Cambridge University. . . .

As we read on, the impression grows that we are being taken on a sentimental journey; and if the book lacks the champagne sparkle of Sterne's garrulous prose, it bubbles at least like soda water: a beverage that some people are reported to like more than others. The patter is maintained throughout, and habitual readers of gossip columns will like the book immensely: it is a sort of molecular Cholly Knickerbocker. They will be happy to hear all about the marital difficulties of one distinguished scientist,[2] the kissing habits of another,[3] or the stomach troubles of a third.[4] The names are preserved for posterity; only I have omitted them here. Do you wish to accompany the founders of a new science as they run after the "Cambridge popsies"? Or do you want to share with them an important truth? "An important truth was slowly entering my head: a scientist's life might be interesting socially as well as intellectually."

In a foreword to Watson's book, Sir Lawrence Bragg praises its "Pepys-like frankness," omitting the not inconsiderable fact that Pepys did not publish his diaries; they were first printed more than a hundred years after his death. Reticence has not been absent from the minds of many as they set out to write accounts of their lives. Thus Edward Gibbon, starting his memoirs:

> My own amusement is my motive and will be my reward; and, if these sheets are communicated to some discreet and indulgent friends, they will be secreted from the public eye till the author shall be removed beyond the reach of criticism or ridicule.

But less discreet contemporaries would probably have been delighted had there been a book in which Galilei said nasty things about Kepler. Most things in Watson's book are, of course, not exactly nasty—except perhaps the treatment accorded the late Rosalind Franklin—and some are quite funny; for instance, the description of Sir Lawrence's futile attempts to escape Crick's armor-piercing voice and laughter. It is a great pity that the double helix was not discovered ten years earlier: some of the episodes could have been brought to the screen splendidly by the Marx Brothers.

As we read about John and Peter, Francis and Herman, Rosy, Odile, Elizabeth, Linus, and Max and Maurice, we may often get the impression that we are made to look through a keyhole at scenes with which we have no business. This is perhaps unavoidable in an autobiography; but then the intensity of vision must redeem the banality of content. This requirement can hardly be said to be met by Watson's book, which may, however, have a strong coterie appeal, as our sciences are dominated more than ever by multiple cliques. Some of those will undoubtedly be interested in a book in which appear so many names, usually first names, that are known to them.

This is then a scientific autobiography; and to the extent that it is nothing else, it belongs to a most awkward literary genre. If the difficulties facing a man trying to record his life are great—and few have overcome them successfully—they are compounded in the case of scientists, of whom many lead monotonous and uneventful lives and who, besides, often do not know how to write. Though I have no profound knowledge of this field, most scientific autobiographies that I have seen have given me the impression of having been written for the remainder tables of the bookstores, reaching them almost before they are published. There are, of course, exceptions: but even Darwin and his circle come to life much more convincingly in Mrs. Raverat's charming recollections of a Cambridge childhood than in his own autobiography, remarkable a book though it is. When Darwin, hypochondriacally wrapped in his shivering plaid, wrote his memoirs, he was in the last years of his life. This touches on another characteristic facet: scientists write their life's history usually after they have retired from active life, in the solemn moment when they feel that they have not much else to say. This is what makes these books so sad to read: the eagerness has gone; the beaverness remains. In this respect, Watson's book is quite exceptional: he is twenty-three when the book begins and twenty-five when it ends; and it was written by a man not yet forty.

There may also be more profound reasons for the general triteness of scientific autobiographies. *Timon of Athens* could not have been written, *Les Demoiselles d'Avignon* could not have been painted, had Shakespeare and Picasso not existed. But of how many scientific achievements can this be claimed? One could almost say that, with very few exceptions, it is not the men that make science; it is science that makes the men. What *A* does today, *B* or *C* or *D* could surely do tomorrow.

Hence the feverish and unscrupulous haste that Watson's book reflects on nearly every page. "Then DNA was still a mystery, up for grabs, and no one was sure who would get it and whether he would deserve it. . . . But now the race was over and, as one of the winners, I knew the tale was not simple. . . ."[5] And later: "I explained how I was racing Peter's father [Pauling] for the Nobel Prize."[6] And again: "I had probably beaten Pauling to the gate."[7] These are just a few of many similar instances. I know of no other document in which the degradation of present-day science to a spectator sport is so clearly brought out. On almost every page, you can see the protagonists racing through the palaestra, as if they were chased by the Hound of Heaven—a Hound of Heaven with a Swedish accent.

There were, of course, good reasons for the hurry, for these long distance runners were far from lonely. They carried, however, considerably less baggage than others whom they considered, sometimes probably quite wrongly, as their competitors. Quite a bit was known about DNA: the discovery of the base-pairing regularities pointed to a dual structure; the impact of Pauling's α-helix prepared the mind for the interpretation of the X-ray data produced by Wilkins, Franklin, and their collaborators at King's College without which, of course, no structural formulation was possible. The workers at King's College, and especially Miss Franklin, were naturally reluctant to slake the Cavendish couple's thirst for other people's knowledge, before they themselves had had time to consider the meaning of their findings. The evidence found its way, however, to Cambridge. One passage must be quoted. Watson goes to see the (rather poor) film *Ecstasy:*

Even during good films I found it almost impossible to forget the bases. The fact that we had at last produced a stereochemically reasonable configuration for the backbone was always in the back of my head. Moreover, there was no longer any fear that it would be incompatible with the experimental data. By then it had been checked out with Rosy's precise measurements. Rosy, of course, did not directly give us her data. For that matter, no one at King's realized they were in our hands. We came upon them because of Max's membership on a committee appointed by the Medical Research Council to look into the research activities of Randall's lab. Since Randall wished to convince the outside committee that he had a productive research group, he had instructed his people to draw up a comprehensive summary of their accomplishments. In due time this was prepared in mimeograph form and sent routinely to all the committee members. As soon as Max saw the sections by Rosy and Maurice, he brought the report in to Francis and me. Quickly scanning its contents, Francis sensed with relief that following my return from King's I had correctly reported to him the essential features of the B pattern. Thus only minor modifications were necessary in our backbone configuration.[8]

Rosy is Rosalind Franklin, Max stands for Perutz.

As can be gathered from this astonishing paragraph, Watson's book is quite frank. Without indulging in excesses of self-laceration, he is not a "stuffed shirt" and seems to tell what he considers the truth, so far as it concerns the others. In many respects, this book is less a scientific autobiography than a document that should be of interest to a sociologist or a psychologist, who could give an assessment that I am not able to supply. Such an analysis would also have to take account of the merciless persiflage concerning "Rosy" (not redeemed by a cloying epilogue) which goes on throughout the book. I knew Miss Franklin personally, as I have known almost all the others appearing in this book; she was a good scientist and made crucial contributions to the understanding of the structure of DNA. A careful reading even of this book will bear this out.

It is perhaps not realized generally to what extent the "heroes" of Watson's book represent a new kind of scientist, and one that could hardly have been thought of before science became a mass occupation, subject to, and forming part of, all the vulgarities of the communications media. These scientists resemble what Ortega y Gasset once called "the vertical invaders," appearing on the scene through a trap door, as it were. "He [Crick] could claim no clear-cut intellectual achievements, and he was still without his Ph.D." "Already for thirty-five years he [Crick] had not stopped talking and nothing of fundamental value had emerged." I believe it is only recently that such terms as the stunt or the scoop have entered the vocabulary of scientists, who also were not in the habit before of referring to each other as smart cookies. But now, the modern version of King Midas has become all too familiar: whatever he touches turns into a publicity release. Under these circumstances, is it a wonder that what is produced may resemble a Horatio Alger story, but will not be a *Sidereus Nuncius?* To the extent, however, that Watson's book may contribute to the much needed demythologization of modern science, it is to be welcomed.

3. Preface to a
Grammar of Biology

Darwin's *Origin of Species,* probably one of the most influential books in the history of science,* was published in 1859. The loud-mouthed, pompous, and insincere admiration of natural science, so characteristic of our time, began much later. It was, for example, possible for wise old Peacock, who in his youth had been Shelley's friend, to let two of the principal figures of his last novel, published in 1860, converse as follows:

> *Lord Curryfin:* . . . We ought to have more wisdom, as we have clearly more science.
> *The Rev. Dr. Opimian:* Science is one thing and wisdom is another. Science is an edged tool with which men play like children and cut their own fingers. If you look at the results which science has brought in its train, you will find them to consist almost wholly in el-

---

*Biological hypotheses are in general accepted by the public much more readily and rapidly than chemical or physical discoveries. Thus, the index to the Schlechta edition of Nietzsche's works records thirty-three references to Darwin, one mention each of Robert Mayer and Virchow, and none of Helmholtz, Clausius or Liebig. In his enormous receptiveness, Novalis is a great exception among German thinkers.

ements of mischief. . . . The day would fail, if I should attempt to enumerate the evils which science has inflicted on mankind. I almost think it is the ultimate destiny of science to exterminate the human race.[1]

Now that we have come so much nearer to this destiny, who would still dare write thus? It is not pleasant to be denounced by dark times as a *vir obscurus*. Still, Jean Paul took this risk in his "War Declaration Against the War," part of that odd and wonderful book whose publication cost so much trouble; 137 years before the explosion of the first atom bomb:

> And who can guarantee, seeing the immense developments in chemistry and physics, that there will not be finally invented an infernal engine which similar to a mine will start and terminate a battle with one shot; so that the enemy can do no better than to deliver the second, and towards evening the entire campaign is finished?[2]

I should like to start this essay with one of the quiet in the land, with Friedrich Miescher, who in 1869 discovered the nucleic acids, somehow between Tübingen and Basel. As was to be expected, nobody paid any attention to this discovery at that time. The giant publicity machines, which today accompany even the smallest move on the chessboard of nature with enormous fanfares, were not yet in place. Seventy-five years had to pass before the importance of Miescher's discovery began to be appreciated. For that it required the appearance of another quiet man whom I shall mention soon.

II

I should like to place these brief remarks under the protection of two sayings. The first comes from an ancient Greek poet who is being credited with the invention of the iamb, Archilochos from Paros, who said: "The fox knows many things, but the hedgehog one big thing."[3] The second word comes from Kierkegaard who in 1849 noted in his diary: "A single man cannot help his time, he can only express its collapse."[4] I use the first saying in reference to Miescher; the second applies to our time. It is more than a hundred years ago that Friedrich Miescher discovered the nucleic acids. First from the nuclei of lymphocytes, and later from the spermatozoa of the Rhine salmon, he was able to isolate what we now would designate as DNA. Miescher himself—and this appears clearly from his correspondence and from the tone of his compact papers—was well aware of the importance of his observations.[5] They failed, however, to make much impression on his time; and how little echo there was can perhaps be deduced from the fact that even today the best history of the natural sciences, in the volume devoted to the nineteenth century and published in 1961, mentions the name of Darwin thirty-one times, that of Huxley fourteen times, but Miescher not at all.[6] There are people who seem to be born in a vanishing cap. Mendel was one of them, and Willard Gibbs and David Keilin, and so also was Miescher. None of them was a fox, and Archilochos would not have hesitated to classify them as hedgehogs.

It is almost impossible to retrace the course of the history of science to an earlier stage, for not only should we be required to forget much of what we have learned, but much of what a previous epoch knew or believed to know has simply never been learned by us. We must remember that the natural sciences are as much a struggle *against* as *for* facts. Every thirty years a new growth makes the old forest impassable. Hence, I shall not even attempt to depict the scientific and intellectual climate in which the first faltering steps of biochemistry occurred. It is, in general, true of every scientific discovery that the road means more than the goal. But only the latter appears in the ordinary scientific papers. Probably, this is mostly to be welcomed, since otherwise there would be no end to the chatter. In the case of Miescher, however, we should have liked to know more. The decision to investigate the chemistry of the cell nucleus testifies to an unusual foresight, but also to a bold disregard of the consequences with which too fast a pioneer must reckon.

A few years ago, I attempted to describe this dilemma facing the scientific outsider, and each pioneer is *eo ipso* an outsider.

> The natural scientist is often faced with a series of observations, a set of phenomena, into which he attempts subsequently to introduce some sort of chronological or causal order. He determines several points and connects them to a curve; he measures certain values in a number of samples and estimates the averages and deviations; he constructs a reaction chain or postulates a cycle: whatever he does, there remains much darkness between the few points of light. Whether he emphasizes the light or dwells on the obscurities will depend upon his temperament, but even more upon the temper of the times and upon a form of ever-changing vogue or fashion which acts as a censor forbidding him to be ahead by more than one or two steps. If he runs too fast, he disappears from our sight; if he goes too slowly, he joins the eighteenth century. For most people, this is not a problem: they are where all the others are.[7]

This is exactly what Miescher did not do: he did not find himself, when he began and also when he ended, where all the others were; and for this reason, only very few paid him the attention that he deserved. One might ask, however, how many of the world-shaking discoveries bestowed on us in the last ten or fifteen years will prove worthy of centenary remembrances. This brings us to a problem in the value theory of science—in what actually constitutes the value of a scientific observation—and these are considerations that I should prefer to avoid here.* What makes the

---

*I should like to venture one remark. One gains the impression that nowadays the value of a piece of research is being measured in terms of its potential for productive unemployment relief: he

study of nature so magnificent is its very givenness: it is because it is; it is as it is; and *tolle, lege!* (pick up and read!) remains its eternal admonition.

In the case of the nucleic acids it is not at all difficult to describe the significance of their discovery. Quite apart from their important biological functions, recognized within the last thirty years, which I shall mention later, the nucleic acids are unique among the four principal classes of cellular constituents—proteins, nucleic acids, lipids, and polysaccharides—in that their discovery can be dated precisely. Here is *one* man, *one* place, *one* date; and this man is Friedrich Miescher (1844–1895). He died young. The frontispiece to his collected papers shows a fine and shy, perhaps a sad face; as if the shortness of his life had thrown a shadow over it. I have often asked myself what such a man would have done in our ghastly time.

The discovery of DNA by Miescher was followed soon after by the description of RNA in the laboratory of Hoppe-Seyler in Tübingen. Then began the long road—in this case nearly eighty years—which every biologically important, complicated chemical substance must travel: first its structure, then its function. Since the nucleic acids are extremely complicated structures, composed of a very large number of four or five simpler substances, the gradual advance of our knowledge progressed somewhat differently, namely in

---

who gives something to do to the greatest number of idling scientists is a great man. For this purpose we have now, for instance, a citation index from which one can ascertain how often he has been cited by others. This is a worthless standard: Meissonier and Bouguereau certainly were mentioned, and bought, more often by their contemporaries than Cézanne and Sisley. If, on the other hand, the value of a scientific observation is to be appraised on the basis of its unexpectedness, its originality, this requires a distance in time, a sort of bird's-eye view. This is true of the sciences no less than of the arts. We only have to think of the lack of appreciation with which Jean Paul or Hölderlin were treated by Goethe and Schiller; except that a scientific Hölderlin would not even have achieved a publication. Unappreciated geniuses in the natural sciences remain unrecognized; for them there is no posterity.

three principal stages: 1) investigation of the primitive structure, that is, identification of all chemical substances that participate in the architecture of the macromolecule; 2) formulation of their biological functions as carriers of genetic information; 3) recognition of their species-specific character and of their detailed structure. This work was carried out by many, and there would be little sense in offering a list of all their names. However, a few names should be mentioned. In the first stage there were, following Miescher and Hoppe-Seyler, Piccard, Kossel, Altmann, Neumann, Jones, Steudel, Feulgen, P. A. Levene, Thannhauser, Hammarsten, Jorpes, Gerhard Schmidt, Dische, and Gulland. In the second stage, in addition to Brachet and Caspersson, there was Avery. In the third stage there was myself, Wilkins, Crick, and Watson. Many different personalities were involved, different temperaments, different characters; and the many little chips that they unearthed gained significance and color only in the mosaic of the whole.

The generally ant-like character of the natural sciences is made particularly evident in this history; only now the ants have become rather more obtrusive. (Watson's *The Double Helix* depicts the hectic climate of present-day research quite adequately.) Also, we deal less with a mosaic than with a jigsaw puzzle in which it is not necessary for all pieces to fit perfectly, as long as the image, expected or permitted by present-day opinion, is reproduced approximately. The so-called exact sciences often are not as exact as is commonly believed. How often they infer the existence of a hat from the emergence of a rabbit! Nowadays it is not rare for an intensive search, or only an intensive assertion, to produce what looks like truth: this is what could be called *veritas creata* (created truth). But there is something much higher, namely, *veritas creans* (creating truth).

III

At this point, I should like to indulge in a short digression. Nature can be explored on many levels; none is more or less profound, none is more or less correct, but they are different. Which one you choose depends upon inclination, talent, accident, but most of all, unfortunately, upon fashion. Now one could say, at the risk of some superficiality, that there exist principally two types of scientists. The ones, and they are rare, wish to *understand* the world, to know nature; the others, much more frequent, wish to *explain* it. The first are searching for truth, often with the knowledge that they will not attain it; the second strive for plausibility, for the achievement of an intellectually consistent, and hence successful, view of the world. To the first nature reveals itself in lyrical intensity; to the others in logical clarity, and *they* are the masters of the world. Goethe was certainly wrong and Newton right; but somehow I cannot escape the feeling that, as long as humanity lasts, the dispute will never be entirely resolved. The laughter of Spinoza, as he watched two spiders battling each other, can still be heard. It is almost an intrinsic part of our concept of science that we never know enough. At all times one could almost say that we can explain it all, but understand only very little.

Most scientists, therefore, are what Archilochos would have called foxes, and they know many things. And then there still is a subdivision, much on the rise in biology, and these wish to *change* the world. (This is surely not the kind of change contemplated by the young Marx in his eleventh Feuerbach thesis.) With them I do not wish to deal here, for I am convinced that the attempts to improve or outsmart nature have almost brought about its disappearance; just as the all too frequent performance of intelligence tests is more likely to make the testers more stupid than the tested more intelligent. That the end sanctifies the means has for more than a hundred years been the credo of the sciences; in actual fact, it is the means that have diabolized the end.

IV

Physiological chemistry, still in its infancy, was the first science to become interested in the nucleic acids; somewhat later, organic chemistry, already highly developed at that time, took up the study. The constituents—the purines and pyrimidines and their sugar derivatives which form the actual components of the nucleic acids, *i.e.*, the nucleosides and the nucleotides—were isolated and characterized. Better methods for the isolation of the nucleic acids from tissues were developed. And, finally, rather complicated studies led to the identification of the two sugars, deoxyribose and ribose, which are characteristic of the two types of nucleic acid. At a still later date there began the synthetic and analytic work which was followed by the description of several more or less specific enzymes. Earlier I mentioned the principal names of those that participated in this work. Now I should like to add the names of several organic chemists who took part in the first basic attempts at synthesis: Emil Fischer and Traube, Wheeler and T. B. Johnson, and, much later, Alexander Todd.

What was known about nucleic acids at the end of this stage? Much and little. Their qualitative composition was more or less understood; that is, it was possible to give a list of the types of molecules which were liberated by the degradation of the nucleic acids. These were in the case of DNA: 1) deoxyribose, a pentose sugar; 2) two nitrogen-containing substances belonging to the purine group, adenine and guanine; 3) two related nitrogenous substances belonging to the group of pyrimidines, cytosine and thymine; and finally 4) phosphoric acid. RNA was found to be very similar to DNA in its ultimate constituents. It contains: 1) another pentose, ribose; 2) the same two purines as DNA, adenine and guanine; 3) two pyrimidines, of which one is identical with a DNA constituent, cytosine and uracil; and again 4) phosphoric acid.

Further work demonstrated that in the nucleic acids each of the purines and pyrimidines carries a sugar moiety— these derivatives are called nucleosides—and that each nucleoside carries a phosphate; these nucleoside phosphates are designated as nucleotides. This is then the primary structure of a nucleic acid: a chain of nucleotides linked to each other via phosphate bridges, a polynucleotide. It will simplify the following discussion if a few simple abbreviations are introduced, namely, the initials of the various purine and pyrimidine nucleotides. In speaking of A, G, C,

T, or U we designate the corresponding nucleotides containing adenine, guanine, cytosine, thymine, or uracil. For many decades the formulation of a DNA looked very simple, for instance: $(AGCT)_n$. One postulated the existence of a compound composed of all four building blocks, a so-called tetranucleotide, which was repeated several times in a nucleic acid. No firm assertion could be made as to the size of this value n, though it was considered quite small. The notion of the occurrence of giant molecules, polymers, even in the living cell, prevailed only slowly, first perhaps with regard to the proteins. How enormous the leap into the present actually is may be seen from the fact that the molecular weight of a chain composed of ten tetranucleotides is about 12,000, whereas now the molecular weights of various DNA species are computed as many millions, and even billions. If the nucleic acids are viewed as a text, it could be said that in less than thirty years a short aphorism has grown into an immense epic.

Although it was known that both nucleic acid types, DNA and RNA, occur in all living cells, no conception of their function, nor even of their actual structure, had emerged.

V

This brings us to a period, seventy-five years after Miescher's discovery, to the year 1944. At that time there appeared a publication by Avery and collaborators on the mechanism of the so-called Griffith phenomenon, the transformation of one pneumococcal type into another. The final sentence of this remarkable paper, which was disregarded in the widest scientific circles, reads as follows: "The evidence presented supports the belief that a nucleic acid of the deoxyribose type is the fundamental unit of the transforming principle of Pneumococcus Type III.[8] As this transformation represents a permanently inheritable alteration of a cell, the chemical nature of the substance responsible for this alteration had here been elucidated for the first time. Seldom has more been said in so few words. The man who wrote them, Oswald Theodore Avery (1877–1955), was at that time already sixty-seven, a rare instance of an old man making a great scientific discovery. It had not been his first. He was a quiet man; and it would have honored the world more, had it honored him more. What counts, however, in science is to be not so much the first as the last.

This discovery, almost abruptly, appeared to foreshadow a chemistry of heredity and, moreover, made probable the nucleic acid character of the gene. It certainly made an impression on a few, not on many, but probably on nobody a more profound one than on me. For I saw before me in dark contours the beginning of a grammar of biology. Just as Cardinal Newman in the title of a celebrated book, *The Grammar of Assent*, spoke of the grammar of belief, I use this word as a description of the main elements and principles of a science. Avery gave us the first text of a new language, or rather he showed us where to look for it. I resolved to search for this text.

Consequently, I decided to relinquish all that we had been working on or to bring it to a quick conclusion, although the problems were not without interest and dealt with many facets of cellular chemistry. I have asked myself frequently whether I was not wrong in turning around the rudder so abruptly and whether it would have been better not to succumb to the fascination of the moment; but these biographical bagatelles cannot be of interest to anybody. To the scientist nature is like a mirror that breaks every thirty years; and who cares about the broken glass of past times?

I started from the conviction that, if different DNA species exhibited different biological activities, there should also exist chemically demonstrable differences between deoxyribonucleic acids. From the very beginning I drew an analogy to the proteins in assuming that the biological activity of the nucleic acid probably rested on the sequence specificity of its constituents—on the order in which the four different nucleotides were arranged in the macromolecule—rather than on the occurrence of new, as yet unrecognized constituents. The prototype of this difference then would be *Roma-Amor* and not *Roma-Rosa*. This has proved to be correct.

There existed, however, a difficulty which appeared almost unsurmountable: the lack of any method for the precise chemical characterization of a nucleic acid. The development of suitable procedures took two years, 1946–48. The results were most surprising. They showed that the old and unfounded tetranucleotide hypothesis was wrong; that there existed an enormous number of different deoxyribonucleic acids whose composition was constant and characteristic within the species and within all organs of the same species. In other words, the different DNA species differed from each other, as is the case with the proteins, through the different arrangement of their constituents, through different nucleotide sequences. This was, strictly speaking, the beginning of the notion, so commonly accepted in the meantime, of the "information content" of DNA.

Retaining the previously defined abbreviations, a DNA molecule could no longer be formulated as $(AGCT)_n$ but as $(A_mG_nC_oT_p)$, with m, n, o, p representing not only very high values, but values characteristically different in DNA preparations isolated from different species. This placed the nucleic acids for the first time on the same level as the proteins.

But there emerged also something much more surprising, which distinguished the nucleic acids from the proteins, namely, a sort of equipoise between the several DNA constituents that had not yet been observed in any other natural polymer. This is the relationship between adenine and thymine on the one hand, guanine and cytosine on the other, which I first called complementarity; but several years later, under the name of "base-pairing," it became the fundamental slogan of a new science. These observations were reported in several lectures in 1949 and published at the beginning of 1950.[9]

These were the observations: if the total formula of a DNA molecule is written as $(A_mG_nC_oT_p)$, we find in many differently composed DNA species that the values m and p are equal, as are the values n and o, and that the sums $(m + n)$ and $(o + p)$ show equality as do the sums $(m + o)$ and

$(n + p)$. To put it in words, the DNA constituents are paired as follows: 1. adenine with thymine; 2. guanine with cytosine; 3. purines with pyrimidines; 4. the substances classified chemically as 6-amino derivatives (adenine and cytosine) with the 6-oxo derivatives (guanine and thymine).

VI

The natural sciences are furiously writing on second volumes of which there exist neither the first nor the last. Nothing is ever finished in this slippery world. But the second volume containing the observations outlined above can be considered concluded. In referring to this work as historical I use a synonym for oblivion.

Before turning to the further course of our history I should mention a second subterranean branch of the great river for which unfortunately nobody has come up with a more sensible name than "molecular biology," namely, the early work on bacteriophages, principally *E. coli* phages. The names of Delbrück and Luria, S. S. Cohen, and Hershey are connected with these studies.

These investigations on viruses had the merit of making available simple and clearly perceptible systems. Many studies would have come to nothing had they been limited to plant or animal cells or only to bacteria. Like every reformation this too was a deformation; it has served to push the major part of research into an area of which it is not even clear whether it represents a microcosmic image of living nature. What happens so frequently in the natural sciences has happened again: depth engenders restriction. In the end, we know nearly everything about nearly nothing.

What was essential in these findings was the demonstration that the proliferation of bacterial viruses in the infected bacterial cell is mediated solely through the DNA of the phages. These results, therefore, confirmed Avery's previously mentioned seminal observations.

What has, consequently, become evident is that DNA, at least under certain conditions, can be considered the carrier of "biological information", that this information must be based on sequence specificity, and that the DNA molecules are distinguished by peculiar and unusual regularities of their composition. The newer history is again connected with a series of names, of which a few should be mentioned: Watson and Crick, Monod and Jacob, Holley and Nirenberg. But this newer history of biology is also connected with something else, and this could form the subject of an apocalyptic intermezzo.

VII

In the last fifteen years we have witnessed an event that, I believe, is unique in the history of the natural sciences: their subjugation to and incorporation into the whirls and frenzies of disgusting publicity and propaganda. This is no doubt symptomatic of the precarious position assigned by present-day society to any form of intellectual activity. Such intellectual pursuits have at all times been both absurd and fragile; but they become ever more ludicrous when, as is now true of science, they become mass professions and must, as homeless pretentious parasites, justify their right to exist in a period devoted to nothing but the rapid consumption of goods and amusements. These sciences were always a *divertissement* in the sense in which Pascal used the word; but what is their function in a society living under the motto *lunam et circenses?* Are they only a band of court jesters in search of courts which, if they ever existed, have long lost their desire to be amused?

End of the World through Black Magic was the title Karl Kraus gave to one of his books. (His time was, compared with ours, still bucolic; but the great prophets always live in the future.) The black magic of our days—these mass media concerned with both the production and the distribution of so-called news; these forever titillating and nauseating intimacies, splashing all over us from newspapers and magazines, from radio and television; this bubbling and babbling emptiness of deadened imagination—has taken hold of science, as of all other intellectual products of humanity. They have swallowed it up. It is easy to understand why today's youth experiences a revulsion from all these synthetic celebrities strutting on the television screens of the world, from the ever increasing pollution of our intellectual and our actual atmosphere. And if, at least in America, the students begin to develop a distinct aversion to the natural sciences, this is certainly due in part to the fact that these sciences appear to form part of the discredited trappings of a hated history. Hiroshima is more than the name of a destroyed city.

Since the end of the second world war—but especially since the Russian successes in space flight—the financial resources, particularly in the United States, being pumped into the natural sciences, have increased in a manner that would have been unimaginable before. This has given rise to a popularization, but also to an enormous vulgarization, of science. Its achievements have begun to take on the form of a spectator sport, and young scientists start like race horses. Science has been perverted by public opinion to a sort of Hollywood and it has begun to adapt itself to this brutal standard. The noise, enormous even before, has increased with the restriction of available funds.* The old joke about the conversation between two Pavlovian dogs could be modified slightly: "Every time I ring the bell a guy comes and gives me a prize."

Still, it is surprising that in such bad times—somehow between Auschwitz and Vietnam—so much good science has been produced. I do not know, though what to conclude. (Times not so bad, sciences not so good?) That in our days such pygmies throw such giant shadows only shows how late in the day it has become.

---

*Often, especially in the field of virus and phage genetics, quite banal discoveries are celebrated with a newspaper and television ballyhoo that would have deserved a better soap. Although these are mostly pseudo-discoveries, not even applicable to unicellular organisms, one uses press conferences, interviews, etc. to allude to the imminent "synthesis of life" or to impending cures by "genetic engineering." The public, which forgets rapidly, retains the pleasant taste of the greatness and vigor of the sciences.

VIII

On the basis of the X-ray work on DNA by Wilkins in London and the chemical observations of my laboratory, Crick and Watson in 1953 made a very fruitful proposal with respect to the macromolecular architecture, the secondary structure, of DNA.[10] This model—a double helix consisting of two intertwined DNA strands held together by specific hydrogen bonds, namely those predicted by the above mentioned principles of base-pairing—forms an important part of the grammar that the title of this paper has alluded to. It is, in any event, the most intelligent explanation of the regularities discovered by us: of base-pairing, the equivalence of purines and pyrimidines, etc.

The model of a double-stranded DNA immediately suggested a possible pathway for nature to bring about the replication of a DNA molecule with the conservation of its innate biological information, based on its nucleotide sequence. The old strand A makes the new strand B, the old strand B makes the new strand A; positive makes negative, negative makes positive, and so on *ad infinitum*. This process has been realized *in vitro* enzymically; but the living cell, with its confounded multidimensionality, still presents many question marks. Nevertheless, one may say that the problem of the *conservation* of hereditary biological information is relatively well understood, though it is less true of the mechanisms through which such information can be changed. The insight into the *transmission* of the text coded into DNA, *i.e.*, its transcription into complementary RNA and the translation of this RNA into different proteins, encounters greater difficulties and these processes are understood only in vague outlines. The first step consisted in the demonstration of enzyme systems (RNA polymerases) which, with the use of a DNA as an obligatory template, are able to synthesize RNA molecules of complementary composition and nucleotide sequence.

These RNA molecules belong to several different classes. We encounter here, among others, the comparatively high-molecular species of ribosomal RNA, then the small molecules of transfer RNA, at least one type for each of the amino acids occurring in proteins, and finally a very large number of different so-called "messenger RNA" molecules—substances that transmit the instruction of the DNA concerning the structure of enzymes and other proteins to the ribosomes where the synthesis of proteins takes place. Each of these messengers carries the cipher for at least one protein, read from a section of the DNA of the genome. The RNA of plant viruses and certain RNA-containing bacteriophages presumably contains the code for several proteins whose synthesis is induced by the infection.

From all this, and from many other things for which I have no room to discuss here, we have learned that the range of what is considered as biological specificity is always in danger of being underestimated. If DNA is really our thread of Ariadne, the labyrinths out of which it is expected to lead us are truly inscrutable. When in biochemistry we employ such an innocuously sounding expression as, for instance, that a certain protein, an enzyme, "recognizes" a specific nucleotide sequence, do we as much as suspect how much of an anthropomorphic hypostatization we have undertaken?

All the schemes, which in several versions represent the "central dogma"—"DNA makes RNA and RNA makes protein"—would not have carried us far had it not been possible to demonstrate, more or less conclusively, that RNA really contains nucleotide triplets, each of which form the code word for a given amino acid, as, *e.g.*, UUU for the amino acid phenylalanine. I do not wish to discuss here how valid these assignments really are, but prefer to limit myself to admiring the magnitude of the cryptographic achievement, rejoicing in the fact that nature seems so much better than Shakespeare whom Dr. Johnson reproved for not having been able to write "six lines together without a fault."

IX

These then, sketched with reprehensible superficiality, are the elements which made possible the first step to a "gram-

mar of biology." If the French saying, "Il n'y a que le pre-
mier pas qui coûte," were correct, the rest ought to be easy.
In other words, today the smallest of the small bacteriophages, tomorrow the brain that conceived *Die Zauber-
flöte*. But in my laboratory there exists an old proverb: "The
first success in an experiment comes from the devil; but
then the way drags on." And truly, it will still take a long
time to get from the relatively primitive structures, such as
phages and viruses, with which molecular biology is principally concerned, to the higher unicellular organisms, let
alone the multicellular ones.

Total knowledge requires a limited universe, but the
realm of life has no boundaries recognizable to us except
death itself. The consequence of this is that life, since we
cannot define it, has as a category practically disappeared from modern biology. We are really still very far
from an actual grammar of the living cell, not to speak of a
grammar of an organ, an organism or, even more, a thinking organism. It is not by accident that the grammar of the
tower of Babel was not written. The processes of cell differentiation, morphogenesis, and cellular organization still
are entirely obscure. One could almost say that we have
remained as far from the goal as ever. For our goal is still to
understand nature, not to talk it to death.

Do we really understand the world? We designate what
we understand as the world. Humanity has an enormous
capacity to disregard the incomprehensible. There are many
peculiar expressions found in our journals. A phage is said
to "commit suicide," an infected bacterial cell to "abort." I
myself may have been heard to say that a nucleic acid chain
is being read, copied, or even translated—that it is the carrier of biological information, of a message acquired
through transcription and transmitted as a translation. Are
not these all expressions which, if we try to think them to
their end, make the epistemological twilight of our sciences
appear even more livid? We posit intelligence where we
deny it. We humanize things, but we reify man. I am afraid
that our sciences have not escaped the process of alienation,
of dehumanization, so characteristic of our time. The at-

tempt to describe life in its generalized contours leads to an automatization before which everything—the leap of the cat or the Goldberg Variations—appears equally incomprehensible.

In the study of biology, the several disciplines exist next to each other, but they do not come together. We have no real idea of the inside of a living cell for we lack what could be called a science of compressed spaces, we lack a scientific knowledge of a whole; and while a sum can be subdivided, this is not true of a whole. I know full well that science progresses from the simple to the complex. I, too, have been taught that one must begin at the bottom; but shall we ever emerge at the top?

I look out the window. There is a dog; he barks, he wags his tail. What is his molecular biology? The new normative biology has won great triumphs and caused great damage. By its readiness to explain all, it has blinded us to the fact that we understand little. It has furnished us with the key to a very small lock; but the door it has opened for us, is it perhaps merely a door to a castle in the air? Somehow I cannot rid myself of the feeling that we still lack an entire dimension that is necessary for the understanding of a living cell; and I am not thinking of the *vis vitalis*.

Our biology, no less than our technology, is a product of capitalism, governed by unwritten rules of supply and demand. Just as the ones poke around the moon, the others ransack life. The slogan always is: *Eritis sicut diaboli, scientes bonum, facientes malum* ("Ye shall be as devils, knowing good, doing evil"). I believe, we have not reflected sufficiently on the real goals of these new natural sciences. When I began my studies the battle cry was "knowledge"; now it is "power." It was much later that I discovered that in 1597 Francis Bacon had already announced the identity of these goals. But what is "power" in biology? The type of answer I get promises, for instance, the production of heaps of thoroughly healthy Einsteins. But is this desirable? Who will sew the pants for these Einsteins and, still more important, who will write the newspaper articles about them? But, really, these are only jokes. Since not even the most primitive of the smallest bacteriophages has been un-raveled, this type of debased creation will still require much time; and warners and offenders will have been buried long before in one and the same Nirvana of oblivion. Perhaps —but I have little hope—humanity will in the meantime have become more intelligent.

Faced with this enormous throng of sorcerer's appren-tices, I should like to add only one remark. It seems to me that man cannot live without mysteries. One could say, the great biologists worked in the very light of darkness. We have been deprived of this fertile night. The moon, to which as a child I used to look up on a clear night, really is no more; never again will it fill grove and glen with its soft and misty gleam!* What will have to go next? I am afraid, I shall be misunderstood when I say that through each of these great scientific-technological exploits the points of contact between humanity and reality are diminished ir-reversibly.

---

*This passage alludes, of course, to the first lines of Goethe's cele-brated song, "An den Mond." *Füllest wieder Busch und Tal/Still mit Nebelglanz.* . . .

4. Bitter Fruits from the Tree of Knowledge: The Current Revulsion from Science

I

I have been a scientist for many years; and although I have always tried to maintain my amateur status, it is still true that I have spent most of my life in the laboratory doing one thing or another. It is, therefore, not difficult to understand why I am concerned by the widespread revulsion of science that is noticeable among our young people and quite a few older ones. This aversion often takes the form of a distaste for scientists, for "experts," for people licensed to have an opinion on a narrowly defined set of matters that the rest of humanity really cares very little about.

This beautiful soft rug on which we have been playing our games for such a long time, has it been pulled from under us? Or have we pulled it ourselves? What makes all this so surprising to us is that we had been under the illusion that the name of this rug was Nature. How could objections be raised to studying what we all felt ourselves to be part of? Dignified indignation assumes a posture resembling that of Jan Hus on the way to the stake; the cry *Sancta simplicitas!*, ascribed to him on a similar occasion, is designed to make us feel like victims of what is often referred to as the current wave of anti-intellectualism. I do not believe that anti-intellectualism is stronger now than before. What I think has happened is that, while people always lived *by* their wits, not so many expected to be paid *for* their wits; and that the present overproduction of professional intellectuals* has caused a certain amount of disgust for this peculiarly undefinable specialty.

The point I shall try to make is that something has gone wrong with our ways of doing science, and even with the views, held by a majority of scientists, about what the purpose of studying nature in all its manifestations really is.

II

"Nature" comes from the Latin word *natura*, she who will be born or she who will bear. [Adherents of the women's lib movement should be happy to hear that "nature" is feminine in many languages: in Greek and Latin, in French and Italian, in German and Russian.] But for the first time in human history we may begin to ask ourselves: "Will she always be born or are we approaching the time when, perhaps, she will be born no longer?" The great old goddess Cybele, is she on the pill? Even worse, is she on drugs? Has the defoliation of the human mind made such progress that soon the only thing that still can grow, will be misery? This, too, is one of the bitter fruits: our *magna mater* has become the *cloaca maxima*.

But Cassandra feels happier looking back to the past than into the future, and even there her jaundiced eye discerns peculiar signposts. Our modern sciences began, one could say, about 350 years ago, in the late Renaissance. Soon we hear from Francis Bacon, and he proclaims in 1597: "Knowledge is power." Then there rises out of less ancient dust the majestic and bearded figure of the great historian Lord Acton, and he says to me: "Power corrupts and absolute power corrupts absolutely." At which moment the logical machinery begins to grind: *Science is knowledge is power cor-*

---

*This sort of professionalism is recognized and honored by the newspapers through the use of the definite article when such celebrities—people who are known to be known—are mentioned: J. S., *the* medical scientist; M. M., *the* anthropologist; Jack, *the* ripper.

rupts. And the young scholastic may raise his hand and blurt out the conclusion: "*Absolute science corrupts absolutely!*" "Thank you," says society, "but nobody asked you. And anyway, Lord Acton was a Catholic, and we all know since the expulsion from Paradise that God is strictly anti-science; had Adam and Eve remained where they were, the wheel would not yet have been invented."

But, one must ask in all seriousness, can knowledge and science be equated? Or is science only a subdivision of human knowledge? Is a certain reluctance to eat all the eggs that science has laid really a revolt against the intellect? One of G. Lukács' best books is entitled *Die Zerstörung der Vernunft;* it deals with the ferment, the destruction of reason, that preceded—as cause and symptom—the collapse of much of Western society into fascism. Would Lukács also have subsumed what I am here talking about—more a revulsion than a revolt—under his general verdict? Well, maybe he would; but he would have been mistaken, as he sometimes was.

Altogether, the cult of smartness has in our time reached exaggerated proportions. Now that even the bombs have become smart—lasers guide them to where the killing is best—many of our young people may have decided that this is not the kind of smartness to which they aspire. The present scene may strike them as swarming with two-minute eggheads.

Although there may be no unanimity about the extent of the territory covered by science, and not even about its purpose and definition, most of us will agree that "science" usually now stands for the knowledge of nature or the search for such knowledge. Science thus certainly does not comprise all the knowledge that the human mind can comprehend; but at its highest, for instance, when it derived general laws of nature,* science has seemed to past cen-

---

*I am certain that the majority of scientists will say that nature obeys certain laws. Actually, I would say, it is the laws that obey nature. St. Thomas Aquinas said it better, though in a different context: *Ratio imitatur naturam.* (Reason imitates nature).

turies to carry a spark of divinity. Listen, for instance, to
Johannes Kepler:

> There is nothing that I should desire to know more
> than this: God, whom I can almost touch with my
> hands when observing the universe, do I find him also
> in myself?

> Only the love of truth can work miracles.

> I wanted to become a theologian, and I was long
> restless. But see now, how God through my labors is
> being celebrated even in Astronomy.

> There is nothing more miraculous, nothing more
> beautiful, nothing that more clearly demonstrates the
> wisdom of the Creator, than the movements of the five
> planets.

Surely, the music of the spheres must have sounded like
Palestrina to this man who was truly what Novalis said
about Spinoza: drunk with God, *gotttrunken*.

This, then, is one kind of scientist; and I doubt that we
shall see anymore of these. Even Galilei, certainly a great
man and much more the prototype of what was to follow,
was very different; and in the way he neglected to give
credit to Kepler, he was very much a man of our time.

One could almost say that the first great scientists considered themselves mediators between man and eternity, reeds
trembling in the great winds of God; they seemed to belong
to a sort of sainthood—they were *practical saints*. But even
then, some people must have asked themselves: "Can this
be reconciled, practical and saint?" As time went on, practicality increased and sainthood vanished. This must have
been prefigured in prehistory: the first genius invented the
wheel, the second sold it. This is my entirely unacceptable
etymology of the American epithet of admiration: "a
wheeler-dealer."

III

It is certainly not an accident that the upswing of science
coincides with the end of feudalism, with the loss of abso-

lute power on the part of the church; that it was born as the Middle Ages died. The Renaissance and the Reformation, the printing press, the beginning of capitalism, the great voyages of exploration, the discovery of America, this tremendous breaking-through of walls that surely were not only walls of constraint but also walls of protection—they all were witnesses to the birth of modern science. Science is, in many ways, a child of early expansionist capitalism. A sober, unsentimental observer could regard it as an imperialistic assault on nature, an attempt to colonize nature as if one were dealing with a newly discovered and highly exploitable continent.

The human mind in its long history has given rise to many different creations. There is philosophy and theology; there is music and painting and sculpture, architecture and literature; there are the "humanities" and law; and there are mathematics and the natural sciences. In the Middle Ages—a much more civilized period than our bestial century, for no king then declared Attila "a great Hun" or advocated the vandalization of a country—when you went to school, you studied the seven liberal arts: the *trivium* taught you grammar, rhetoric, and logic; the *quadrivium*, arithmetic, music, geometry, and astronomy. Having learned all this, you were an educated man. But unless you became a teacher yourself, there was no particular practical use of all this wisdom; you just possessed it.

The abominable idea that "knowledge is power" came much later. But even Francis Bacon would not have been ready to accept the nexus between the knowledge of chemistry and the power of Napalm.

It was, hence, at the time of the Renaissance when things began to be lively. The corruption, consequence of power, suddenly became noticeable. Listen to one of the founders of Renaissance philosophy, the Florentine Marsilio Ficino:

> Who could deny that man possesses almost the same genius as the Author of the heavens? And who could deny that man could somehow also make the heavens,

could he only obtain the instruments and the heavenly material?

Well, I for one would deny it; but I like the "somehow." It contains much of the future Mr. Fix-it spirit of our sciences. It also foreshadows the element of arrogant redundancy, so characteristic of our times; for who needs a second heaven? Though Ficino may remind you of NASA, even he might have hesitated to suggest, as was done not long ago, the explosion of a small atomic bomb on the moon, just to see what would happen. This modest proposal came, of course, from a geologist. Incidentally, the fact that American feet in American-made rubber galoshes first desecrated the "eternal silence" of the firmament obviously has made the moon into an experimental object of NASA. Will the Hubris Corporation, the biggest U.S. conglomerate of the twenty-first century, be exploiting the universe?

That science knows no boundaries was looked upon by older times with comic surprise; and in Dickens' *Bleak House* there appears briefly another geologist, a gently amusing eccentric:

> "People objected to Professor Dingo, when we were staying in the North of Devon, after our marriage," said Mrs. Badger, "that he disfigured some of the houses and other buildings, by chipping off fragments of these edifices with his little geological hammer. But the Professor replied that he knew of no building, save the Temple of Science!"

Surely, the Temple of Science has become full of funny priests in the meantime! Incidentally, the application of science may have always gone along with arrogance, exaggeration, and impudence, but certainly never more than in our day. Where could such braggarts be found before?*

But let me return to science and its beginnings. We are

---

*Did not President Nixon declare after the first moon landing that this was "the greatest week since the Creation"—presumably after agreed, I hope, that science can be defined as the *inductive* search for truth about nature. The other form, the *deductive* search for truth, I am not competent, or at any rate not called upon, to discuss. The search for truth is certainly one of the oldest and purest motives of the human intellect (although it is debatable whether the inductive reasoning of science—based much too often on two experiments that give more or less similar results—really leads to truth or only to probability, let alone plausibility). Also, I cannot solve what may be a riddle to many of us, namely why, during most of human history, the common man has found his consolation neither in inductive nor in deductive truth, neither in science nor in philosophy, but in *revealed* truth, in religion, which speaks out of deeper and more mysterious layers of the human mind than does reason.

Science, or what is often called pure science, then, is without doubt a noble occupation of the intellect; a nobility that I should hesitate to extend necessarily to its practitioners, the scientists. Yet, this is not the attitude toward science that will be found to prevail among the majority of mankind. There are many people who do not care for poetry, music or art; but I do not think they hate them. On the other hand, I have often encountered a true revulsion from science. And this is not a recent aversion; many examples can be found in the older literature. Humanity hates nothing more than to feel the ground, on which they no longer stand firmly, being undermined. As long as they stood firmly, they did not mind. But there is more. It is quite clear that the blessings of pure science are not as obvious to the common man as are the benefits of other fruits of the human intellect. He feels instinctively that *Don Giovanni* or *Die Kritik der reinen Vernunft* or the *Divina Commedia* belong to another category. They are not so all-invasive; he does not have to hear or read them if he does not want to. He has not learned the difference between science and technology;

---

having his White House aides make a careful examination of all the weeks since the Creation to make sure that there had not been an even greater one?

he will get more pleasure from music, painting or literature than he will derive from, say, the Second Law of Thermodynamics or the discoveries of Darwin and Mendel, colossal as these may be.

And then there is another thing: the awful remoteness of science from the mainstream of human thinking. Everything has to be taken on trust; there is no real popularization possible, only a vulgarization that in most instances distorts the discoveries beyond recognition. One often hears it said that science has developed its own language. This is not true. The sciences have created many mutually unintelligible professional slangs, so that a biologist cannot understand a paper in, say, *The Physical Review,* and a physicist is completely lost in *The Journal of Molecular Biology* or in *Virology.* This means that, outside of his own ever-narrowing field of specialization, a scientist is a layman. What members of an academy of science have in common is a certain form of semi-parasitic living.

IV

Earlier I mentioned the difficulty of distinguishing between science and technology. The fact that this distinction is indeed so difficult to make brings us to one of the cruxes of the problem we are discussing. To say that technology is the applied use of the sciences is not a good definition; but it does point out the difference between science and almost all other intellectual activities—science can be used, and therefore misused, like nothing else. Surely if a Schubert sonata is piped into the waiting room of an airport, or a Picasso painting used to embellish a carpet advertisement, this is not applied music or applied art; it is merely the seal of our barbaric times. But the two greatest technological misdeeds of our days—the atomic bomb and the landing on the moon—are certainly the children, or at least the bastards, of science. *In hoc signo vincetis,* said the Devil to the assembled scientists, and it was not in their dreams; but what a sign, what a victory!

Of the beginnings of science it could perhaps be asserted that they are conceivable, and actually came about, without the help of technology, though this is no longer true in our time. But technology is unthinkable without mathematics, physics, and chemistry. If you want to see how science could flourish in an empire without being degraded by the demands of the industrial revolution, you have only to look at Needham's marvelous books about the history of science in China. Moreover, even technology takes on a very different aspect in societies that are not entirely propelled by greed than in a consumers' and producers' society in which the more junk is produced, the more junk is needed. One might say that science has been corrupted by technology and technology in turn by the profit motive, the military, the mass media, and advertising. The dislike of any of these manifestations of our miserable times is likely to turn against science which, perhaps, is no more guilty than were Adam and Eve when they ate an apple to keep the doctor away. Actually, that was when the doctor made his first appearance.

V

It would, however, be shortsighted to blame the neon-light vulgarity of much of our science on the neon lights. There is a flaw inherent in the very fabric of science which remained unrecognized as long as science was undertaken by a minute minority. But when quantity changed, so did quality. Science has always been unable to give more than extremely partial answers to extremely general questions. It was the reverse of the old proverb: the seven wise men asked the questions, and one fool answered; but he never ran out of answers. In the meantime, the often unrecognized piecemeal and provisional character of science has fragmented our world; as if we were called upon to reconstruct the innumerable patterns of a kaleidoscope from a few pieces of colored glass, but without the tube in which they are held in the instrument.

What both critics and admirers of science often tend to forget is that science is not a description of the world, but only an introduction into one of the many ways in which one could go about describing it. It is certainly, among all occupations of the human mind, the one that offers the smallest range of permissible results. Beckmesser would have made a perfect average scientist. Moreover, the kind of questions we ask is conditioned by the kind of answers we expect; and if people—certainly not lured by television into expecting a wide spectrum of spiritual excitation—cannot read in the current *Scientific American* all about the imminent cure of cancer, they are perfectly content with hearing all about the expanding universe. Science has become a *fait divers,* taking its place with the stale bread and the manipulated games that are supposed to entertain the populace.

VI

I have just now mentioned the fragmentation of our world which has been caused by the scientific revolution of the last few centuries. At least, so it appears to me as a scientist. It is possible that people who have not spent their lives in science are not at all aware of this and may even deny it; but then again they could be wrong. At any rate, at the very beginning when it all happened, one great and profound poet knew it and said it. When John Donne wrote *The first Anniversary* he contrasted the view of the world, the Ptolemaean picture, as it was inherited from the Ancients—with its firm earth as the center, its eternal fire, its crystalline sphere, its *primum mobile*—with the universe, created for us by Copernicus, Kepler, Galilei, etc. He wrote:

> And new Philosophy calls all in doubt,
> The Element of fire is quite put out;
> The Sun is lost, and th'earth, and no mans wit
> Can well direct him where to looke for it.
> And freely men confesse that this world's spent,
> When in the Planets and the Firmament
> They seeke so many new; they see that this
> Is crumbled out againe to his Atomies.
> 'Tis all in peeces, all cohaerence gone;
> All just supply, and all Relation. . . .[1]

This is one of the few indications that have come to my attention that there existed people who understood that it was not only for petty motives that there were a few who were not happy about Galilei's dwelling in "the Temple of Science." They knew that the cry *fiat scientia et pereat mundus!* did not come from the mouths of angels.

VII

I should now like to introduce you to what I call the "Devil's doctrine." It says: *What can be done must be done.* This innocent-sounding and useful maxim—it abolishes with one stroke all problems of conscience and free will—is of comparatively recent origin. Even during the industrial revolution, when the unholy marriage between science and technology was consummated, the brutalization of the scientific imagination, so characteristic of our time, progressed only slowly. But for some time science has been operating under this doctrine.

Let me give you two examples. The first comes from Leonardo da Vinci. It is often said that he kept his discoveries secret, lest they be misused for warfare. This is not quite true; as a young man he wrote a letter to Ludovico Sforza offering his services and describing his skill in constructing war machines. But what is true is that later in his life, when he kept his copious diary, he sketched a design for a submarine and wrote:

> How and why I do not describe my method of remaining under water for as long a time as I can remain without food; and this I do not publish or divulge on account of the evil nature of men who would practice assassinations at the bottom of the seas by breaking the ships in their lowest parts and sinking them together with the crews who are in them.

My second example comes from more recent days. Chlorine gas was known since 1774 and phosgene, $COCl_2$, since 1812. The gruesome effects of these chemicals on the body had been noted, and avoided, by many generations of chemists. They used hoods, they wore gloves and even gas masks when experimenting with these things. Why did it have to wait until 1914 before the idea came to a few chemists that these substances could, and therefore should, be used as weapons? What had happened in these intervening 100 or 150 years? I can pose the question, but I cannot answer it. Since that time, innumerable sophisticated poisons and irritants—and even mutagenic agents—have been squirted at our fellow beings. Never mind whether this is disguised as "insurgency control" or "pacification"; a tear gas smells no better when it is called a "lachrymator." In our time Virgil's *lacrimae rerum* have acquired a new meaning: the things, and not only they, have good reason to weep over this world.

VIII

The rest of these lines will be devoted to one concrete example in which the application of the Devil's doctrine is to be expected and feared. I am thinking of what is vulgarly called *genetic engineering.* It is not so much that I fear the success—there won't be any—but rather that each such attempt, windy and hopeless and barbaric as it may be, lifts our sciences and all of us to an ever higher level of moral entropy.

I can take for granted the scientific basis on which these attempts will rest. Since the discovery of the laws of heredity by Mendel or, rather, since their rediscovery at the beginning of this century, there has been much speculation on the chemical nature of the genes—the inheritable units of the hereditary characters—and on their localization within the cell. The latter was ascertained long before the former; and there now is more or less general agreement that the genes are in the main situated in the chromosomes of the cell nucleus, whereas the cytoplasm, the area surrounding the nucleus in the cell, plays an as yet not well-understood accessory role in heredity. Then, in 1944, the celebrated paper of Avery, MacLeod, and McCarty appeared[2] in which, for the first time, it was made likely that the genes consisted of DNA, deoxyribonucleic acid. Soon afterwards, it proved possible to demonstrate, by chemical investigations, that there existed an enormous number of different nucleic acids, differing in their composition and in the sequence in which their constituents, the nucleotides, were arranged in the extremely long chains which they formed.

In the present jargon of biology, which is (what a paradox!) both anthropomorphic and dehumanizing, one would say that DNA carries the "genetic information" and that it gives "instructions" to the cellular apparatus concerned with the synthesis of proteins, enzymes, etc. The theory also postulates the existence of middlemen, that is, chemical agents that receive the instructions from the DNA and see to it that they are obeyed. These are the ribonucleic acids, RNA.

We have, hence, a truly feudal system: masters that will always be masters, slaves that will always be slaves, and in the middle the clerks of whom *Webster's Collegiate Dictionary* gives the following whimsical definition—"A person who can read, or read and write; a scholar." This relationship has been enshrined in the so-called Central Dogma: "DNA makes RNA makes protein"—a dogma, incidentally, which is no longer accepted. Nowadays our sciences, quick and fickle, wear out dogmas in ten years, and axioms take only a little longer.

In science, attempts at formulating hierarchies are always doomed to eventual failure. A Newton will always be followed by an Einstein, a Stahl by a Lavoisier; and who can say who will come after us? What the human mind has fabricated must be subject to all the changes—which are not progress—that the human mind must undergo. The "last words" of the sciences are often replaced, more often forgotten. Science is a relentlessly dialectical process, though it suffers continuously under the necessary relativation of equally indispensable absolutes. It is, however, possible that the ever-growing intellectual and moral pollution of our scientific atmosphere will bring this process to a standstill. The immense library of ancient Alexandria was both symptom and cause of the ossification of the Greek intellect. Even now I know of some who feel that we know too much about the wrong things.

IX

One other element must be mentioned. This is the principle of base-pairing, discovered about twenty-eight years ago, which has played a very important role in present-day biological thought. It postulates the existence of specific bonds between the various constituents of a nucleic acid. For instance, in DNA the purines pair with the pyrimidines, adenine pairs with thymine, guanine pairs with cytosine. This completely novel principle has led to a generally accepted model of DNA as a double helix, consisting of two strands whose sequences are complementary to each other and which are held together by specific base-pairing. This multiple key-and-lock relationship of base-pairing now forms the basis of our thinking about how DNA is "replicated" by enzymes, how portions of it are "transcribed" to form specific RNA molecules, how these are utilized to direct the synthesis of proteins, etc. And if such terms as "replication," "transcription," and "translation" now are so common in molecular biology, this is due to the general adoption of the base-pairing rules.

In mentioning molecular biology I have referred to a conglomerate representing a fusion of biochemistry, biophysics, genetics, virology, and a few other things. This new industrial giant has had many great successes in the recent past, though its stock has started to decline lately. There are more profound reasons for this decline, but the most obvious one is the disinclination on the part of the money-granting agencies to support unlimited "basic research" and their desire for relevance and useful applications.

And since scientific imagination strays where money beckons, it is no wonder that two key words have come to the fore. They are *genetic engineering* and *cancer*. About the latter I shall have nothing to say here but the former can bear some attention. At first glance, the term sounds very innocent and appeals to the pragmatic character of the American people. Mr. A. is a hemophiliac, and this is due to a defective gene. So, why not replace it? Mrs. B. cannot digest lactose, and this is due to a missing gene. So, why not graft it onto her? Why not indeed? Actually, this is all shameless talk. We still are so far from knowing how this could be done, that it does not pay even to discuss it. In the meantime, one could perhaps point out that a nation that does not know the difference between automobiles and human beings is in danger of mistaking their hospitals for morgues, their jails for extermination camps; and when it bombs peasants, it will call them trucks.

At what time the idea of reconstructing and improving man by genetic engineering first came about, I cannot say. Probably not long before 1963 when a Ciba Symposium with the innocuous title *Man and His Future* took place in London.[3] When I glanced through the book that preserves the proceedings of this conference, I remembered what I said before: "The moment when Caliban turns into cannibal cannot be predicted, but it can be recognized." I feared that the moment had come, for I got the impression that the cannibals had taken over. And I remembered that the Nazi extermination camps also started as an experiment in eugenics. At the risk of being accused of not recognizing the famous Anglo-Saxon sense of humor, I should like to quote a few passages. I leave out the names of the contributors, since some of them may be ashamed of what they then said, and others can no longer be.

Do people have the right to have children at all? It would not be difficult for a government to put something into our food so that nobody could have children. Then possibly they could provide another chemical that would reverse the effect of the first, and only people licensed to bear children would be given this second chemical.

Clearly a gibbon is better preadapted than a man for life in a low gravitational field, such as that of a space ship, an asteroid, or perhaps even the moon. A platyrhine with a prehensile tail is even more so. Gene grafting may make it possible to incorporate such features into the human stocks. The human legs and much of the pelvis are not wanted. Men who had lost their

legs by accident or mutation would be specially qualified as astronauts. If a drug is discovered with an action
like that of thalidomide, but on the leg rudiments only,
not the arms, it may be useful to prepare the crew of
the first spaceship. . . . A regressive mutation to the
condition of our ancestors in the mid-pliocene, with
prehensile feet, no appreciable heels, and an ape-like
pelvis, would be still better.

Now we can define man. Genotypically at least, he is
six feet of a particular molecular sequence of carbon,
hydrogen, oxygen, nitrogen and phosphorus atoms—
the length of DNA tightly coiled in the nucleus of his
provenient egg.

Clearly, to most collaborators of this symposium man appears as expendable as *E. coli* or yeast, as consumable as an
ox, and the most bizarre experimentation is contemplated
and discussed in the old terms of the Devil which I have
mentioned before. It is a document that later times, if there
are later times, will use to show to what depths of barbarism our age had fallen.

You will, perhaps, find that I exaggerate in my horror at
seeing the genetic equipment of man messed around with.
It is true, I have a great suspicion of biological do-gooders.
They begin as reformers and end as murderers, for Frankenstein must always kill his monster. As I said it many years
ago:

> So I have learned to watch these clever fingers closely
> and not to believe the song of the sirens, even if they
> are sirens with a Ph.D. When they tell me: "As soon as
> we have mastered the genetic code, we shall know how
> to cure cancer," my answer is: "Maybe; but before this,
> you will probably succeed in converting humanity into
> a bunch of mongoloid idiots by putting just the right
> amount of base analogues into the DNA."[4]

And then there is the equally shameless and thoughtless
talk about "creating life in the test tube." A few years ago,
an eminent scientist proposed that the creation of life be

made an American national goal. And this at a time when the Army of the United States already was busy destroying hundreds of thousands of lives that had still been created by the antiquated process. I conclude that it is in its imagination that decaying humanity first begins to rot.

X

The impassivity of the cool observer of nature; the statistification, if I may coin this term, of our scientific thinking—perhaps justified when we deal with the number of viable cells or mutants in a bacterial culture—turns into a monstrosity when we are made to listen to the daily recitation of the body count in our eternal battles which are now all under strictly scientific control.

An instance in which scientific detachment merges—for me at least—with sheer horror may be seen in the heart "transplants." The organs—snatched from donors who, at any rate, after the removal of their hearts, are certainly dead—are grafted on to moribund recipients who are most unlikely to survive long enough to begin paying off the surgeon's bill. And all this is done without a shudder, without a feeling for the immenseness of the depths into which the healer's hands intrude; it is all done in the name of science, an impassive study on experimental patients.

One may object that I am really speaking here of medicine, not of science. It is true, whether medicine is the youngest science or the second-oldest profession may be a matter of controversy; but the people are wont to count the achievements of medicine among the triumphs of science, and in some cases rightly so; and we must understand if, owing to its all-pervasiveness, science is blamed for the excesses to which it has contributed.

XI

What has happened, why did the dreams of mankind grow stale and murderous? I am told that life has really become too complex. But why does bestiality increase with complexity? Does science have a share in all this? Science can no longer be said to be a search for truth about nature. It is much rather an attempt to outsmart nature, to repeat a "creation-type experiment," but with "American know-how." Quite apart from the fact that, owing to general decay, this claim is no longer justified—I often speak of the "American knew-how"—is this really what so many great scientists have given their lives to bring about?

In our time, the goals of science have become distorted, and science itself has become overgrown with much heartless arrogance and aloofness; qualities that some people may feel reside less in the profession than in its practitioners. This has given rise to a widespread revulsion from science, especially among young people. In many respects I regret this, though I know that society has the science it deserves.

But there is, beyond this, a deeper-seated revulsion—or should I say, a shudder—that is shaking science itself. Not long ago, I read the fascinating correspondence between Einstein and Max Born.[5] Especially toward the end of their lives, it is moving to notice how a sort of horror begins to appear between the lines, a terror at what physics in its cursed marriage with technology has produced. All these profound geniuses, these gentle mathematicians, meditating in their well-lit and widely visible ivory laboratories—and then, suddenly, before their windows, Hiroshima and Nagasaki!

In our times, we have been led to forget what human conscience and human responsibility really mean. We have begun to believe that the mere fact that something can be done carries its own justification. The individual scientist certainly will not agree with the view I have taken. After the atom bombs had exploded over Japan many horror-stricken physicists turned their spiritual pockets inside out to show that nothing impure was hidden there; but to no avail. In hell, everybody works for the devil!

XII

I do not want to end with hell. In one of her books, that poor and wonderful woman, Simone Weil, whose thoughts and aphorisms are like tiny splinters of a shattered paradise, writes the following words:

> La science, aujourd'hui, cherchera une source d'inspiration au-dessus d'elle ou périra.
> La science ne présente que trois intérêts: 1° les applications techniques; 2° jeu d'échecs; 3° chemin vers Dieu. (Le jeu d'échecs est agrémenté de concours, prix et médailles.) [6]

If we consider that this was written more than thirty years ago—long, long before the "smart bomb," the "electronic battlefield," the "heart transplants"—the precision of the concept may surprise us, though it will strike ninety-nine percent of all scientists as absurd or, at least, bizarre. The distinction between practicality and the exercise of trickiness, apparently proposed as the definition of "pure science," may still be understandable; but what of the third possibility offered? Does Simone Weil suggest a return to Kepler, a man who never wrote a grant proposal? I do not know the answer; but I wonder how many will agree with me that the way we have been going cannot continue much longer.

What then is the remedy? I have no real answer—I should have to write an entire book to reveal my ignorance—nor am I entitled to advocate Simone Weil's third solution. Clearly, a cosmetic improvement of the "image" of science will be useless; no singing commercials, which may have deodorized many a deodorant, or elected a President, will help.

What is more necessary than ever is a clear concept of what science can do and what it cannot. Science is certainly not a substitute for religion or philosophy. It is a way to investigate, not to define, reality. How inept scientists are in defining reality can, in fact, be seen in several recent mock philosophical books which read as if they had been written by one of Ionesco's rhinoceroses. Also, the news that astronauts had failed to encounter God during their flights had better remain unpublished. Surely science is not a way to explore the unexplorable.*

I am rather doubtful that regulatory legislation can do much good; but genetic manipulation should be proscribed, and novel experiments on patients should not be permitted before the doctors have experimented on each other. A general cooling of the overheated production of so-called scientific facts would be helpful; this, too, is a form of inflation that no human institution can withstand forever. The sciences, like other professions, cannot endure if their practitioners are unable to know more than an ever smaller portion of what they must know in order to function properly. Computers may be faster than the human brain, but they cannot replace it. In all times, science has grown through unforeseeable analogies, through unpredictable strokes of imagination.

It must, however, be clear that the ordering of science presupposes an ordering of human society, and that this demands a revolution of a dimension hard to imagine. Even the end of the second millennium—only so few years away—cannot induce me to attempt an outline.

The great pendulum of birth and death; the darkness and mystery of human destinies; the great concepts that for many thousands of years spoke to the mind and even more to the heart of humanity—reconciliation and charity, redemption and salvation—have they all been pushed aside and annihilated by science? I do not believe so. But if it really were the case, then science would carry a guilt even greater than its most embittered detractors have asserted.

---

*It is surprising to me that I know of no grant proposal to determine the average weight of the soul by accurately weighing large numbers of dying people before and after death has occurred.

5. Building the Tower of Babble

I

"Two weeks later," Watson writes in his book *The Double Helix*, "Chargaff and I glanced at each other in Paris. A trace of a sardonic smile was all the recognition I got when we passed in the courtyard . . . of the Sorbonne."[1] Unfortunately retaining, as I do, only the trivialities of my past, I remember the incident at the Biochemistry Congress in 1952 and the gawky young figure, so reminiscent of one of the apprentice cobblers out of Nestroy's *Lumpazivagabundus*. I felt far from sardonic. I was looking for a toilet; but whatever door I opened, there was a lecture room and the same large portrait of Cardinal Richelieu.

"Sarcastic" or "sardonic" are the attributes usually accorded me in that book. But what I really was, when I first met the fervid pair in Cambridge, was baffled, for here were two people trying to fit the nucleotides into a helix and worrying about its pitch—it became a double helix, I believe, after I had told them about our results—without bothering to look up the structures of the compounds they wanted to fit together. My dismay before so much unimpeded boldness will be understandable only to those who consider that at that time molecular biology did not yet exist. In the meantime the sciences have learned that it is profitable to transgress their boundaries and to overreach their competence. Somehow they swallow more than they have bitten off. So perhaps "laconic" would have been a better attribute, for what I jotted down when I left Cambridge was: "Two pitchmen in search of a helix."

II

It is, however, not of Watson's book that I want to speak; I have done this in an earlier part of this book. What I should like to do is to sketch in a few words how it felt to get into science, and especially into the field of the nucleic acids, in those prehistoric times (B.W.C.), before revelations had begun coming down from the mountains; before the "invisible colleges" had begun to play their disagreeable roles as restrictive guilds; and, for that matter, before scientific journals had begun to sprout sprightly little feuilletons. In addition, I should like to say a few words about how the present scene strikes me.

No one who has entered science within the last thirty years or so can imagine how small the scientific establishment then was. The selection process operated mainly through a form of an initial vow of poverty. Apart from industrial employment, important for a few scientific disciplines such as chemistry, there were few university posts, and they were mostly ill-paid. One of my chiefs at that time assured me that for him the opportunity of doing research as he pleased was sufficient recompense. (He had, besides, a comfortable private income.)

Science—or at any rate that part of science with which I am familiar—was small; it was cheap; it was wide open. One could still do experiments in the old fashioned sense of the word. Now, everybody is working away at "projects" whose outcome must be known in advance, since otherwise the inordinate financial investment could not be justified. Papers, however, continue being written in the old way, as if the discovery had come after the search. The number of very significant scientific discoveries made in the interval between the two world wars was truly enormous. The impulse persisted, or even increased, in the United States up to about 1950 or 1955, and then slackened perceptibly, almost in reverse proportion to the number of new scientists entering the several disciplines. I know of few instances in which the dialectical change of quantity into quality has been so obvious.

Since at that time it cost relatively little to perform scientific experiments, it was always possible and even inviting to venture into fresh areas. The risk was minimal and so, unfortunately, were the results sometimes. But the road to them was always delightful. This changed gradually owing to several powerful technological advances. The introduction of isotopic labels gave rise to an industry whose products became increasingly more expensive, as the variety of the compounds grew and purity standards declined. The construction of powerful centrifuges and other physical equipment greatly extended the range of the possible, but even more the cost of achieving it. Other advances, especially in chromatography, electrophoresis, and spectrophotometry, contributed more than they took away. Still it remains that according to my highly unreliable estimate a current paper of mine costs about twenty to twenty-five times more to produce than an equivalent article did thirty-five years ago, if such things can be weighed and compared. The argument that such calculations are meaningless—for, what would we give if we had one more Mozart opera?—can be rejected; none of us writes Mozart operas.

III

The small number of scientific workers engaged in research had other consequences. It was easy to open new fields and to go on cultivating them; there was no fear of immediate dispossession as is bound to happen now. There were relatively few symposia, and those were not attended almost exclusively by hungry locusts yearning for fields to invade. Bibliographies were comparatively honest, whereas now entire packages of references are being lifted by a form of transduction, as it were, from one paper to the next; so that if some work gets into the habit of not being quoted, it never will be so again. The break in the continuity of the tradition has, perhaps, been one of the most disastrous effects of the scientific mass society in which we are living now. The illusion that what is new is true has distorted the very sense of scientific research. The urge to be "with it" is incompatible with the search for truth about nature—and that is what science is—and where you can say "this is no longer true," there nothing is true. Some years ago, I heard an eminent colleague declare at a congress: "The results that I reported last year were based on facts that are no longer available"—a form of recantation that should have delighted Galilei without offending the Inquisition. Our current literature is brimming with facts, but many, I am afraid, are no longer available. If the vaunted self-purification of science has broken down some time ago, this is only in part due to the ever-increasing complexity of ever more poorly described experiments. It is even more due to the pressed and driven mood in which research often is performed now—" . . . in a hurry of waste, and haste, and glare, and gloss, and glitter" (Byron, *Don Juan*, 10, 26).

Two more points will complete this hasty sketch of a Golden Age that never was. As the number of scientists was so small, it was easy for a young man to establish himself. Two or three decent papers, and he was in, for what it was worth. Another consequence of the restricted dimensions of our scientific knowledge at that time, before it was overwhelmed by multiple massive explosions of facts, many of them of the utmost triviality, was that it was still possible to comprehend the essentials of one or even several sciences. This bucolic security has, I believe, ended—"out of swimmers we have all turned into floaters."[2] Or, as I have put it less metaphorically, "the sciences, like other professions, cannot endure if their practitioners are unable to know more than an ever-smaller portion of what they must know in order to function properly." Even granting all the present difficulties in acquiring sufficient knowledge, I must say that the extreme dislike, and therefore ignorance, of chemistry I have often encountered among molecular biologists are puzzling. Chemistry is the science of substances; and to the extent that molecular biology deals with substances and not in them, as if they were commodities, a thorough acquaintance with chemistry is advisable.

IV

I should be sorry if I give the impression that I am trying to paint an *aurea aetas*. I grew up in bestial times, and they have become worse. Earlier, I expressed my surprise that such bad times gave rise to so much good science; probably the only activity of the human mind that has, until recently, been in the ascendant. It is, however, not astonishing that in a rotten society even the saints will carry a slight aroma of rottenness.

One of the outstanding curses of my lifetime has been the manipulation of mankind by advertising and propaganda. In the sciences this evil force had for a long time remained unnoticeable, perhaps because the expanding capitalism and the youthful imperialism had other worries, perhaps because scientists owing to their small number survived unharmed in the crevices of a society that still paid little attention to them. The first figure of the highest rank that I saw being lifted by the wheels of the publicity machine and turned into a celebrity was Einstein. (Einstein's very interesting correspondence with Max Born and also with Mrs. Born displays many instances of this process.[3] Compare, for instance, the letters of 7 and 13 October, 1920, pp. 62 and 65). Freud, who could have been another victim, escaped the glare entirely, being twenty-three years older. He also benefited from the fact that his discoveries were relatively accessible; an element of impenetrability helps. There may have been, before my time, another instance of mindless acclaim, namely, in the case of the Curies and the discovery of radium, to judge at any rate from the slightly paranoiac image reflected in Strindberg's *Blue Books;* but then one could hardly have spoken of the mass media.

However, at the time when molecular biology appeared on the scene, the publicity machines were all in position and it was time for the saturnalia to begin in full force.

V

I should not want to leave the impression that molecular biology began with the double helix. The reason, and even the date, of the appearance of sectarian movements is hard to determine. I have, in another article, attempted to delineate its pedigree which probably had its origin in the discovery of the transforming properties of DNA and the introduction of bacteriophages as objects of biological research. In my opinion, there really was little sense in creating a new science that consisted essentially in the application of chemistry, and to a limited extent of physics, to biology; that is what biochemistry and biophysics stand for.

I remember vividly my first impression when I saw the two celebrated notes on DNA.[4] The tone was certainly unusual: somehow oracular and imperious, almost decalogous. Difficulties, e.g., the even now not well-understood manner of unwinding the huge bihelical structures under the conditions of the living cell, were brushed aside, in the Mr. Fix-it spirit that was later to become so evident in our scientific literature. It was the same spirit that soon after brought us the "Central Dogma" to which I believe I have been the first to register my objection, never having been very fond of gurus with a Ph. D. I could see that this was the dawn of something new: a sort of normative biology that commanded nature to behave in accordance with the models.

The structural model proposed for DNA in the first note,[5] a helical dyad held together by base-pairing, appeared to me not only as an aesthetically pleasing solution, but also as the most plausible inference from the base-pairing regularities earlier discovered by us in many DNA preparations.[6] I was much less in agreement with the scheme for DNA replication proposed in the second note[7]; and even now, twenty years and thousands of experiments later, I cannot say that I am reconciled with it completely, the mechanism of DNA synthesis *in vivo* still being obscure to me.

I do not know whether in 1865, when Kekulé put forward

the structural model of benzene, which was to revolutionize organic chemistry, neckties appeared forthwith, embroidered with the pretty hexagons. I should rather doubt it, since at that time mass cretinization had not yet begun and advertising still was a home industry. At any rate, the publicity carnival that ensued upon the unveiling of the DNA model was probably unique in the history of science. I have given a brief description in my Bertner Foundation Award Lecture.[8]

VI

Scientific induction is actually the resultant of a parallelogram of rational and irrational forces. That is why in many respects Science is not a science, it is an art. The importance for scientific research of imagination, of unpredictable conclusions from unexpected analogies can, therefore, not be overestimated. If all can be declared in advance, then there remains only the dull verification. The greater the reliance on axiomatic constructions, on prescriptive models must be, the more restricted becomes the freedom of the scientific intellect, and the narrower is the range of what can be discovered. There are, I am afraid, the conditions under which a great part of molecular biology now operates.

Research always runs the danger of overasserting the truth of its observations, leaving ever less space for dialectics to turn around. For me, however, scientific truth consists of what has not yet been disproved; it is at best a dense mosaic of approximations. Therefore the chase is worth so much more than the prey; or, to put it less violently, the road counts more than the destination. Do I hereby propose Sisyphus as the patron saint of the scientist? Not in a general way. What was tragic about the fate of this mythological celebrity was that he was always lifting and losing the same rock; which is, indeed, what many molecular biologists are now doing.

Many of the papers in this field are very competent technically. Since the same procedures are used, regardless of the particular biological system investigated, the results usually confirm each other; and this is taken to prove the unity of nature. When novel apparatus and techniques are introduced, a new set of results is obtained; and this is registered as scientific progress. A pall of monotony has descended on what used to be the liveliest and most attractive of all scientific professions. The noble study of botany, for instance, has been all but banished from many universities. Before, the biological sciences had their characteristic faces and their distinct spheres of interest into which they drew different types of scientists. Now when I go through a laboratory, be it of virology or developmental physiology, there they all sit before the same high-speed centrifuges or scintillation counters producing the same superposable graphs. There has been very little room left for the all-important play of scientific imagination. *Homo ludens* has been overcome by the seriousness of corporate finances.

VII

Our period, just because it is so intellectually weak, is given to extraordinarily strong assertions. Many of the great constructions of our time—existentialism, structuralism, transformational grammar, the central dogma and some other sloganized tenets of molecular biology, etc.—have all looked, from their very beginning, somehow shoddy and overblown. There was about them a flavor of not being entirely earned, as of trick images viewed in a mirror. As the mirror clouded over, the images vanished. Much of what they claimed may actually have been true; but they looked like packages much too large for what they contained. One got the impression that it often was the wrapping that produced the particular content; just as there are now packaging artists who wrap entire mountains in plastic flimsy.

This is not the note, however, on which I wish to end. I should like to recall a few names. They are the names of those who had done some of the basic work on nucleic acids and whom I got to know personally, either before or after I left sweeter fields to concern myself with the harsh problems of nucleic acid chemistry. It was T. B. Johnson of Yale University who first got me to America; he had done some of the most important work on the chemistry of the purines and pyrimidines. I met Steudel, once one of Kossel's collaborators, at the University of Berlin. Alexander Todd showed me through the organic chemistry laboratories when I visited Oxford in 1934. I often saw P. A. Levene at the Rockefeller Institute; his work, especially on the sugar constituents of the nucleic acids, deserves more admiration than it now receives. At the same institute I sometimes got a glimpse of the great and modest Avery. And there were Gulland and Jordan and J. N. Davidson, Brachet and Caspersson, Bawden and Pirie, Astbury and Bernal, Hammarsten and Jorpes, Thannhauser and Gerhard Schmidt, Mirsky and Pollister, and the gentle and courteous Belozersky in Moscow. Zacharias Dische, without whose diphenylamine reaction most of the work on DNA could not have been performed, has for years been a colleague at Columbia University. Many of these men have gone, but the list is, luckily, not entirely sepulchral. They all did their work before the stripmining of nature had become so prevalent, before researchers had become alienated from the objects of their study. In the tower of forlornness, which the House of Science has become in my time, the inhabitants all speak the same language, but do not understand each other.

Few will be of my opinion, certainly not the one who made fun of me some time ago in a magazine article, saying that my ideal of a scientist was Louis Pasteur played by Paul Muni. This may be so, though I doubt it. What I do dislike, however, is to see *E. coli* impersonating nature. The difference in talents is really too great.

6. Profitable Wonders

In Praise of Uselessness

The title of this essay is taken from the first lines of the *Centuries* of Thomas Traherne. This great religious poet of the seventeenth century can hardly be suspected of following, in his Britishness, a premature Benthamite line. He was thinking of other wonders and other profits. Trying to beat immediate rewards even out of the miracles of the human intellect has been left to our times, which look at science as if it were a stockyard of the mind. There may be plenty of wonders in what science can reveal—but profits? I have never been ashamed of proclaiming the essential uselessness of science. There have been, of course, occasional and accidental blessings; but, on the whole, the uses that men have drawn from science have contributed to their misery. It has made them too strong for their wits. Maybe a wiser species could have prevented the mischief. But the serpent, though promising my primordial ancestors the blue out of the sky and the red out of hell, did not tell them how to get rid of radioactive wastes or how to create energy without consuming it. I should, perhaps, have equipped my title with a question mark.

It is, hence, not surprising that I am not particularly fond of the frequently advanced argument of the usefulness of science. Of course, under our deplorable conditions of scientific funding, where scientists have to sing for their money long after they have lost their youthful voices, my statement must be regarded as subversive. One single bird, and fouling so many nests? "Don't you know," they ask me, "that science must be sold to the people like a lipstick or like an only slightly carcinogenic hair dye?" Well, it is a pity that the search for truth about nature must be peddled with singing commercials. In other times, and even now in other countries, this was or is not necessary. I draw the same consequences from reading a very good scientific paper as from listening to a Mozart piano concerto. They are as they are. To understand nature more fully may fill me with delight; but this is all. Statements of this sort have earned me the reputation of an *enfant terrible*, although I should much rather qualify as a *vieillard misérable*.

Still, it remains that some of the nicest things in this world are useless. I can listen to Beverly Sills without her having to prove that her trills have made me a better man. (And, oh wonder, they may have.) But science, almost alone among the many pure occupations of the human mind, is always called upon to demonstrate its immediate relevance and even necessity. It is a throwback to the ancient Egyptian priesthood without whose humming the Nile could not return. One could ask oneself whether this nefarious utilitarian imperative confronting our scientists has something to do with the astonishing fact that science, in the last few decades, has become preponderantly American science. For, as one of the least inspiring American presidents—and there has been no lack of candidates for this title—has said, this country's business is business.

Tribulations of a Reluctant Prophet

Nobody could have predicted our past. It always happened differently from what the sages, whether disguised as prophets or in more businesslike attire, discerned as foreordained in their hasty models. They saw as progress what was only change, and, at that, vectorially indeterminate change; they declared as dawn what was only the reflection of distant fires. Instant happiness was denied to countless generations long before our times got the mistaken idea that it could be preserved in the deep freeze. Only the prophets of doom were an exception, although even they often were off in their time estimates by several orders of magnitude. The greatest of utopians, such as Thomas More or Campanella, could not compete with the savage fury of a Swift; and it is little consolation that the misery of our days will look bucolic when contrasted with that of the century to come. I have tried to answer at other occasions the question of whether science has contributed to our predicament; the outcome may be that if science has not done so, scientists certainly have.

The disrepute into which science has gotten—and not only with our co-neanderthalers—has many reasons, some legitimate, others frivolous. If some congressmen (women are too bright for that) derive childish mirth from reading aloud funny titles of grant applications, this probably means that they have flunked freshman biology. There is nothing in the world that does not begin to appear ridiculous if you look at it for too long a time, especially, if you know nothing about it. Senator Proxmire could undoubtedly move himself and his colleagues to guffaws of hilarious indignation by reading to them Michelangelo's proposal for the Medici chapel. Still, with the money spent on raising the wrong end of a Russian submarine, 50,000 young artists, writers, musicians or scientists could each have received a grant of $10,000; not to speak of the truly utopian dream that some of this money might have enabled the New York subway to repair its car doors so that they would open and close when needed. Most detractors of science are not bright enough to have the right to dislike or combat it. They know even less about what science is than do most scientists. There now exists an anti-science establishment that is not a bit more appealing than the science establishment iself. Which does not mean that there is not room for profound criticism; but this is not the place to attempt it.

In the adventure of science mankind has set out to solve

riddles that have occupied the mind from its very beginnings. Many pertinent and lucid answers have come forth; but it has remained doubtful whether the answers given were really to the questions asked. We were satisfied with what we got; and if science has often produced answers in search of questions, this, too, was acceptable. There were many waters to fill the great stream of Heraclitus, as long as it kept flowing. Only lately has there been some reluctance on the part of the people to continue paying tribute to the countless tributaries of the stream of science.

The inordinately great weight that science has acquired in our times, the breathless and credulous attention with which it is heeded, the pontifical infallibility that it has come to arrogate, have all placed a responsibility on the scientist that he often finds too heavy to carry. He feels that he is expected to transgress his competence; he is made into a freebooter of nature. The field of evolution, and especially of its biochemical foundations, is particularly rich in examples of this leap from small findings to huge conclusions. Not long ago I read of the claim derived from protein dating that it was only comparatively recently that the chimpanzees, for reasons not stated but easily guessed, branched off the human species—a secession that has obviously been incomplete. The danger in all this is that credulity, once deceived, turns easily into disbelief.

Few scientific subjects have undergone so abrupt a change in "visibility" as the nucleic acids with which I propose to deal. This has occurred in my lifetime. Out of the basement where neglected, intractable, minor curiosities are kept, they have moved into the very center of biological thinking; truly an elixir that has made our molecular alchemists much richer than their medieval predecessors could ever have dreamt of becoming. None of the other plastic constituents of the cell—the proteins, the polysaccharides, the lipids—exhibited so steep an ascent from utter disregard into frenetic attention. Several thousand papers dealing with the nucleic acids are published each year; I should have to read at least ten papers a day to keep on top. This means that there are no authorities left, since only those who have no use for their knowledge can acquire it—doubtless a general predicament of all natural sciences in our days. We are now paying the penalty for our complete reliance on induction. Too many particulars spoil the best universal.

The counterargument that much of what is published is rubbish and does not deserve to be read is not valid in the sciences. Quite apart from the fact that all scientific papers are printed with the pretension of being important—none carries the editors' warning that the content is trivial and may be deleterious to the mental capacity of the reader—it remains that what is bile to one is honey to the other. Where one spark will arise to light an entire universe of associative fuses cannot be predicted. If only best papers were to be published, none would be.

The following lines should be read with this "captation of benevolence," namely, that if it is very difficult to write the true history of the past, it is even less inviting to write the history of the future—and as for the present, well, it does not exist; it is gone as the ink flows from my pen. Still, we have to consider the present before attempting a glimpse of things to come.

The Present Scene

The nucleic acids were discovered by Miescher as components of the cell nucleus a little more than a hundred years ago, remaining a chemical curiosity for more than two-thirds of this period. During this time their composition was clarified and they were recognized as phosphorylated sugar derivatives. The sugars were shown to be either one of two pentoses, D-ribose or 2-deoxy-D-ribose. According to the sugar they contained, one learned to distinguish between deoxyribonucleic acids (DNA) and ribonucleic acids (RNA). Later it was demonstrated that the sugars were linked by phosphate bridges going from the 5-position of one molecule to the 3-position of the adjoining one. At carbon-1 the sugars are connected glycosidically to one of four different nitrogenous substances. In RNA, these are principally the two purines adenine and guanine, and the two pyrimidines cytosine and uracil. In DNA, uracil is replaced by its methyl derivative thymine. The structural elements that must be considered in a discussion of the nucleic acids are: (1) the nucleoside, *i.e.*, a compound between the sugar and one of the nitrogenous components mentioned before, and (2) the nucleotide, *i.e.*, the phosphoric acid ester of a nucleoside. The nucleic acids themselves consist of many such interlinked nucleotides—they are polynucleotides. There existed, however, for a long time a great uncertainty about the size of these polymers.

Since the concept of macromolecular polymers was accepted in chemistry only very slowly and reluctantly, even such long-known classes of compounds as the proteins and the polysaccharides were formulated as loose associations of small monomers. It was, therefore, natural that also the nucleic acids, about which much less had been found out, were so regarded, being written as tetranucleotides or as aggregates of a few of those. It is really remarkable that several generations of scientists, some of whom were certainly not devoid of the ability of thinking profoundly, do not seem to have asked themselves why nature should produce so much meaningless rubbish. But it is highly probable that the very concept of "meaning," *i.e.*, of "information" as it applied to biology, could not have arisen at that time.

Although the science of genetics was progressing, it took very long before it was able to establish contact with a much older science, with chemistry. (Once it did establish contact, the togetherness took on epidemic dimensions, giving rise to remarkable malformations, for instance, molecular biology.) The discovery, in 1944,[1] that a DNA preparation from one variant of pneumococcus could transform another in a stable hereditary fashion, whereas DNA specimens from other sources could not, marked an epoch in the biological sciences; it demonstrated that the deoxyribonucleic acids were related to the genes, if they did not actually represent them, as now seems to be the case. The recognition of the chemical nature of the genome is, in fact, one of the greatest feats in biology. The discoverer, Avery, not honored by the Nobel Committee, is together with Tolstoi and Mendeleev one of the monuments of the vanity of human judgments.

My laboratory could demonstrate between 1947 and 1949 that DNA preparations derived from different species differed considerably in their composition; varying proportions of the same four nucleotides were arranged in the form of enormously long chains. The suggestion that genetic information could rest on sequence specificity of the DNA, that the order in which the nucleotides were arranged could form a text, as it were, was to my knowledge first made in a review article I published in the Swiss journal *Experientia* in 1950.[2]

The same article also discussed the evidence that the tetranucleotide hypothesis was incorrect; that there exists an enormous number of different deoxyribonucleic acids, characteristic in their composition of the species, not of the organ, from which they are derived; that DNA specimens from different species differ in the proportions of their constituents and, therefore, in the sequence in which these are arranged; and, perhaps most remarkably, that the abundance of these nucleotide constituents is subject to several unexpected regularities. These are the well-known base-pairing relationships: equality of adenine and thymine, of guanine and cytosine, of total purines and total pyrimidines, of 6-amino and 6-oxo bases.

These chemical findings, as well as a series of crystallographic observations, finally gave rise in 1953 to the well-known structural model of DNA, a helix composed of two polynucleotide strands held together by base-pairing as mentioned before.

In the last few years we have learned a great deal about the functions of DNA and about the various ways in which it exercises these functions. For instance, in a relatively short time we have accumulated an amazing amount of knowledge about the mechanisms of protein synthesis and about the manner in which the maintenance of the specific amino acid sequence of a given protein is regulated by a specific nucleotide sequence of a segment of the DNA of a cell. But we are still quite deficient in an understanding of the key problem, namely, the way in which DNA is replicated in the living cell. This is indeed the pivot of all our concepts of the conservation of those hereditary characteristics that can be said to be controlled by the genome. Assuming that the DNA of a cell really is identical with its genome, we may think the task of the reproducing cell to be simple. It has to replicate the gene complement faithfully and in its entirety, so that each daughter cell possesses the complete and unchanged hereditary equipment. Our ideas about the comparative simplicity of this task may, however, change if we consider how much is already known of the elaborate safeguards and controls that attend the biosynthesis of a protein molecule. It is, hence, not unlikely that at least as many, and probably more, precautions accompany the biosynthesis of the genome itself. Clearly, the study of enzyme reactions *in vitro* with a stripped and degraded DNA template is a very inadequate model of the complexities of DNA replication in the multiplying and differentiating organism. The logic of our reason is still unable to cope with the dialectics of life.

When using the term "DNA molecule" it is good to remember that we are dealing here with polymers often of so gigantic a size as to defy chemical imagination, not to speak of chemical technique. DNA molecules occur as double-stranded chains or as single- or double-stranded circles having masses ranging from, say, 2×10^9 daltons in bacteria to 10^{11} daltons or bigger in eukaryotes. One cannot say that it has been possible to isolate any of these monsters intact in a pure state. These preparations are unable to withstand the shearing forces encountered during conventional isolation and snap at many places, probably at random. Only much smaller DNA varieties, as they are found, for instance, in bacteriophages, are susceptible of chemical manipulation.

A DNA "molecule," which contains something like 150 million nucleotides in each strand, may be likened to an enormous landscape in which many different events can occur simultaneously in different sites. These events could include replication, transcription, denaturation, *i.e.,* partial or complete strand separation, hydrolysis, and chemical modification. How all these operations are regulated in a meaningful fashion in the living cell, so as to guarantee both the conservation and the expression of its biological information, cannot yet be stated.

In dealing with these huge macromolecules, we have, in some respects, transgressed the boundaries of biochemistry as a branch of chemistry; the chemical definition of a molecule has here lost all its meaning. We are faced with an extremely complicated variant of the quipu of the ancient Peruvians in which the array of a large number of signs is the all-important feature. Whereas, however, the signs of a text are perceived by the intellect, the reading accomplished by the cell must be performed through blind scanning by a large number of enzymes and related factors whose coordination under the conditions of life we are far from understanding. It is, in fact, this unresolved dilemma—text without reader, information without intelligence—that has contributed so much to the conceptual malaise experienced by many biologists who think about these matters.

In all this there are still many other things that far surpass our understanding. If we consider, for instance, a fertilized egg cell, we may assume that it contains a huge DNA molecule, comprising in each of its two strands one hundred million or more nucleotides. These, linked to each other in a specific and presumably invariable sequence, constitute the "program" that predetermines the entire biological future of this cell and of the organism to which it will give rise. They tell me that this is a "text." I am willing to accept this, the more so since I was, perhaps, the first to discuss this possibility. But if this text fills a book of many thousand pages, of which each specifies a definite chemical compound or a biological function, it follows that this text itself must not only have produced the eye reading it, but also the hand, as it were, that turns the pages. We know that the development of an organism follows a strictly regulated time course and that the cells making up the gradually differentiating organs are distinguished by specific differences in their chemical composition. The text, hence, is also its own clock and its own censor; it determines what is being accepted or eliminated and at what time. It is, however, arguable that we should not exaggerate the scientific aspects of entelechy, but instead simply admit that we have not even begun to understand what does take place.

I should like to end this section with a childish allegory. I believe that the DNA may well predetermine the shape and the composition of the "bio-piano," but not the music that is being played on it. I can only hope that with these words I do not become the founder of molecular pneumatology, for I really do not know who makes the music.

A Hesitating Glance at What May Happen

A historian contemplating the future of his discipline could, for instance, say: "We need more information about the role of propaganda in the American War of Independence." Or, perhaps: "We ought to know more about the performance of charitable organizations in France during the years preceding the French Revolution." Having said this, he could proceed to collect the evidence or, more likely, tell his graduate students to do so. This is, however, not the principal way in which the natural sciences progress. For, in contrast to other disciplines of learning, the collection of additional evidence is the most pedestrian part of their functions. What really distinguishes the experimental sciences from all others is that they are wide open. Whatever I predict today could be altered or even annulled by an unpredictable discovery made tomorrow. Only archaeology may, in some respects, be similar. Thus, only the duller portions of the sciences can be delineated in their future course. And even this is precarious, for modern research costs a lot of money; and I have little confidence that this will be forthcoming at the rate to which we have been accustomed in the past. Also the impetuous upsurge, the boundless enthusiasm, the devoted boldness that made the first half of this century one of the greatest periods in the history of science have spent themselves. Scientific research is falling more and more into the hands of entrepreneurs who, although there are exceptions, are on the whole a mindless, money-grabbing lot. The onset of megascience, which we have experienced in the recent past, does not augur well for the future of science.

In thinking about the coming tasks of research on nucleic acids I should distinguish between what ought to happen and what probably will happen. I have, for instance, already alluded to our lack of real knowledge of how the genome of a living cell is replicated. This question, difficult enough in itself, includes an even more formidable one: what is the "template in time" which guides the growing cell in its different stages? If all biological information is indeed contained in the primary structure of the DNA, then not only the composition of all life-essential components must be controlled by the DNA, but also the time of their appearance and disappearance. To me, at any rate, this can only be visualized under the image of a "DNA landscape" which I have briefly sketched before. Synthesis and degradation, expression and modification, rupture and healing must all be coordinated, temporally and spatially, in a pulsation of events that we can barely describe. The amplitude of oscillations that life permits must be regulated with a precision for which we still lack an understanding; a little too much to one side or the other, and the pendulum becomes a wrecking ball.

This alignment of functions is presumably brought about in the cell by a multiple enzyme aggregate which does not survive the normal procedures of extraction. It is not certain that such replication complexes can be isolated, for when we start adding up the various operations which such an aggregate ought to accomplish, we may end up with the entire living cell. There are, in fact, few things in the world before which the biochemist feels as uncomfortable as when he has to deal with life itself.

This brings me to another related problem which is not limited to the nucleic acids, but particularly evident in their case: the coexistence in the cell of so many making and breaking agents. This is certainly a reflection of the dialectics of life; but the Hegel of biology has not yet arisen. We lack a system of comprehension as to the manner in which the various mutually exclusive enzymic functions are brought into play; nor can we describe the way by which the different metal activators or inhibitors available to the cell are channeled into the various enzyme reactions in which they play a role. There are many such instances where the activator of one system is the inhibitor of another one.

Who controls the traffic at this biochemical witches' sabbath, or are all our ideas about the living cell wrong? It is customary to say at this point that "only time will tell"; but time more often forgets than tells. This too is, however, a consolation. No scientist's lifework is really continued when he is dead. Others arise who peddle other wares. The world never runs out of snake oil, but it is always a different snake oil.

Earlier, I mentioned that the chemist still lacks methods of handling intact DNA molecules of very large size. Similarly, the manner in which certain proteins can recognize certain nucleotide sequences very precisely and specifically is entirely unexplained. I could go on listing problems that appear to me worth exploring; but for reasons given in the preceding paragraph there is little likelihood that this is the direction in which research will go. It is much more likely that we shall witness an extension of the molecular nightmares that go under the name of genetic engineering, especially since they have lately been outlawed.

Knowing that the desire to improve mankind has led to some of the most horrible atrocities recorded by history, it was with a feeling of deep melancholy that I read about the peculiar conference that took place recently in the neighborhood of Palo Alto. At this Council of Asilomar the molecular bishops and church fathers from all over the world met to condemn the heresies of which they themselves had been the first and the principal perpetrators. This was probably the first time in history that the incendiaries formed their own fire brigade. The edict published in due course, which lists the various forbidden items, reads like a combined curriculum vitae of the conveners of the conference.

The possibilities of splicing pieces of a DNA into another one, *e.g.*, that of a plasmid, which will now go on reproducing many copies of the insert, will certainly be investigated in all possible directions. The itch to be particularly useful to humanity by introducing such homegrown "genes" into patients lacking them will not be withstood. Whether Frankenstein's little biological monsters will be grafted on successfully, I cannot say, nor what else may be introduced at the same time unintentionally. Were I not so averse to rancid science fiction, I should say that the spreading of experimental cancer may be confidently expected.

But enough of this incubus! It is not impossible that the people of the world are getting tired of our kind of science, practiced so noisily and irresponsibly, and at such an exorbitant cost. Starvation and overpopulation, energy waste and pollution—and how many other plagues out of Pandora's box—will make their combined and terrible weights felt. The distorting mirror of our civilization reflects an image that only the devil can enjoy. I know of few of the greatest achievements of modern science that have not been used to murder or maim. People all over the world must have become aware of the fact that the foremost scientific country of our time has proved life's great enemy. The list of the scientific weapons used in Vietnam—be it for herbicide or homicide—reads like a mailorder catalog from hell. If the entire world is turned not only into one electronic battle field, but also into a proving ground for manmade genetic monsters, every scientist will have to become a murderer.

In previous times one used to speak of man's immortal soul; but this usage has disappeared, although man is conceded a psyche which can be treated lucratively. The only use of the word "soul" that I encounter nowadays is in the form of "soul food." Similarly, the term "philosophy" has vanished from the vocabulary of the scientist. The natural sciences began as a branch of philosophy, as natural philosophy; but they have now completely divorced themselves from their erstwhile philosophical foundations, except for a superficial and mostly unacknowledged adherence to a crude form of mechanistic thinking. We cannot even conceive of a science that does not accept the primacy of experimental proof to which all *a priori* theories must surrender. But this was not always so. At the beginning of our historical epoch, as great a man as Hegel understood very well that it is the firm theory that preconditions the range of the discoverable. He proclaimed the dominance of the correct concept.

> One must start from the concept; and even if it cannot possibly do justice to the "rich variety" of nature, as the saying goes, one must trust the concept, though much that is particular cannot yet be explained. . . . The concept is valid by itself; the particulars will then surely fall into line.[3]

This proud assertion of the precedence of thinking over doing is impressive. Those were stronger times, and they proclaimed *Philosophus supra physicos* (the philosopher comes before the scientist). I cannot help wondering whether this means that, if our concepts were wrong, all that we have been doing is wrong. I have only one consolation: not all scientists started from identical concepts.

7. Triviality in Science: A Brief Meditation on Fashions

I

It has happened more than once that I found it necessary to say of one or another eminent colleague: "He is a very busy man, and half of what he publishes is true; but I don't know which half." Similarly, many people complain that by far too much is now being published in science and that half of it is rubbish; but would they know which half? Since most published papers have gone through some sort of reviewing process, we must assume that at least two referees—usually beginning graduate students in the editor's laboratory or in that of the official referee—have found them worthy. Of course, young Homer is known to nod even more often than old Homer; but we ought to be grateful to all these editors and referees for their truly human fallibility, for a journal containing only jewels of the first water would be too dazzling to contemplate.

What we consider junk is conditioned by our interests. We are very lenient on papers in fields distant from ours and honor them for their unintelligibility. We are very rough on papers related to what we are working on, especially if our names are missing from the bibliography—an omission that, as I have pointed out before, is essentially irreversible, since bibliographies usually are wafted in their entirety from one paper to the next, except for the insertion of the respective authors' own contributions which, if luck has it, may then accompany, plasmidlike, the standard package in its subsequent passages.

Most of us will probably agree that among the publications in the disciplines with which we are familiar some are very good, quite a few very bad, and the majority mediocre. There is, however, less likelihood of agreement as to which particular papers belong to these three categories; and even those articles that I should not hesitate to classify as rubbish may find a few admirers, alongside their own authors, of course. But how about papers that do not achieve publication? I should doubt that there are many, for one of my innumerable maxims has been: "No paper, once written, remains unpublished." Scientific papers possess, it would seem, some sort of *élan vital* that impels them to break through to the public although there can be no assurance that anybody will ever read them.

But how close is the agreement among editors or referees as to which manuscripts ought to be published and which rejected? I am assured by highest sociological authority that it is very close in the physical sciences (ninety-seven percent); and even in the "biomedical sciences," with much wobblier standards, it is reasonably close (seventy-five percent).[1] This is taken to indicate that the various scientific disciplines have evolved strict codes on the basis of which the papers are evaluated. This is certainly true, but only on one level of inspection: manuscripts that are judged to be derived from technically incompetent experiments will be rejected with near unanimity. But even here a warning finger must be raised, Americans are notorious decimal hunters, in love with the newest instrumental and even mental gadgets, and they often do not realize that gadgetry has a way of becoming obsolete much faster than does the solidity of the thought processes. It is, hence, not impossible that a perfectly acceptable paper will not be accepted owing to the absence of the newest style of chromium plating. Exaggerated accuracy has turned into many an idiot's delight.

But there is beyond this a different, and perhaps deeper,

consideration. It has to do with the periodic changes of the manner in which we look at things, of what interests us, and of what we reject. Profundities become trivialities and *vice versa,* and simply to remain in step with one's quinquennium becomes an exhausting task. What is it that keeps us all in an iron corset, as it were, that makes us decide that a newly discovered scientific fact is important or trivial? In other words, what determines the style of our looking at, and into, nature? This will be taken up later in this essay, but I hasten to add that the outcome will be a confession of ignorance. In the meantime a few words may be apposite which I used about ten years ago in my Bertner Foundation Award Lecture.

The fashion of our times favors dogmas. Since a dogma is something that everybody is expected to accept, this has led to the incredible monotony of our journals. Very often it is sufficient for me to read the title of a paper in order to reconstruct its summary and even some of the graphs. Most of these papers are very competent; they use the same techniques and arrive at the same results. This is then called the confirmation of a scientific fact. Every few years the techniques change; and then everybody will use the new techniques and confirm a new set of facts. This is called the progress of science. Whatever originality there may be must be hidden in the crevices of an all-embracing conventional makeshift: a huge kitchen midden in which the successive layers of scientific habitation will be dated easily through the various apparatuses and devices and tricks, and even more through the several concepts and terms and slogans, that were fashionable at a given moment.[2]

II

Some time ago I happened to be shown a report of a so-called study section about a proposal for research support. The application with which they had to deal was actually not very exciting, especially to otherwise easily inflammable young molecular biologists, but it contained some solid biochemistry and could certainly have more than passed muster before a review panel that still included a few experienced biochemists. In addition, it must be understood that most applicants—the word raises visions of barefoot, white-clad graybeards singing hymns of devotion to the various acronymous idols that distribute the gold-plated nuggets—that most supplicants, I should say, would hesitate to dangle exciting things before the eager searchers for truth with immediate cash value of whom many panels are now in danger of being composed. For this reason, as my well-tempered experience has taught me, many grant proposals now consist of the as yet unpublished results of the preceding year, for the only certain future is the past; and, besides, it is harder to rob you of what you have done than of what you hope to do—quite in contrast, incidentally, to other layers of our capitalistic society in which even the humblest mugger would refuse a check carrying next year's date.

In any event, what struck me in this report—quite apart from its haughty and petulant tone, as if they were dealing with a contract laborer refusing, or too stupid, to deliver the expected goods—was one sentence concerning an enzyme which prefers to remain anonymous: "The experiments with "anonymase" are trivial but could conceivably turn up clues as to the function of this enzyme."

Starting from this innocuous, though not exactly sipid, sentence, my meditation could take one of several directions. It could, for instance, dwell on the misery of the present support of scientific research in this country and on the complete breakdown of the selection process by the "peers" who are nobody's peers any more, for in this enormously diffuse *patrie des patrons*, in this godfatherland which science has become in our days, nobody knows very much about anything, except where his bread is buttered and where his cronies sit. But this, except for a few stray remarks, is better left for another article and another occasion.

Alternatively, I could consider the sentence as a whole

and ask how a scientist can condemn an experiment before it is performed. One of my oldest maxims has been, and many of my younger colleagues must have heard it from me *ad nauseam:* "Never say no to an experiment." Although how nature works is read off a model nowadays, it is, in fact, the very unpredictability prevailing at the frontiers of science—and where good scientists work, there are the frontiers—that has made great science possible in the past. Did this jury or, better, injury of driven drivers really forget that the "turning-up of clues as to function" has been one of the principal tasks of biochemistry? Do they not know that the path to the goal contains the goal, and that the latter cannot exist without the former?

III

But what really engaged my attention and made me choose it as the starting point of this modest diatribe was the adjective "trivial"; and in this connection I may also have to say a few things about the fashions of science. It would, of course, have been easy to disregard the whole thing and explain it as nothing more than the normal behavior to be expected of scientists when they are not on their best, *i.e.,* when they are not made to put their names down on the line. Few of us will, after so many years in science, have retained the exquisite sensibility of Andersen's fairy tale princess; and I should probably not even have noticed the whole thing, had it not been for the recollection of an ancient occurrence, the word "trivial" playing the role of a kind of molecular *madeleine.*

Many years ago, we spent some time working on an enzyme that attracted our attention, not only because we were the first to see it, but also because its humble and unobtrusive character made it a candidate for neglect by my more ambitious and successful colleagues. At the same time this enzyme was extremely serviceable in its low-key way, and it made compounds for us that we should have had great trouble preparing otherwise. Besides, in some ways I have always preferred to work on neglected things, as far away from most others as I could.*

I was, hence, not unduly surprised when a long time ago I read a review written by a colleague, known to be eminent, in which he attacked our little enzyme as being of doubtful physiological significance. Although it is notoriously difficult to insert any sort of rebuttal into a scientific paper, editors being even more afraid of polemics than of originality, I succeeded in saying a few words which I believe are worth repeating despite the lapse of many years.

It must, however, be pointed out that it is very difficult to decide what is meant by an important enzyme. The attempt to establish an hierarchical order of nature, if it should be undertaken at all, can hardly be based on popularity contests; nor will appraisals that are often made on teleological, and sometimes on aesthetic, grounds carry much conviction. The plain fact of existence surely should outweigh all these considerations.

IV

It was, then, the word "trivial" that formed for me a bridge between all sorts of associations and made me reflect again on our views of nature and its scientific investigation. I am willing to concede that our civilization, for which life and nature have become a shabby spectator sport, has, under the guidance of the several sciences and of the many other disciplines that would love to be sciences, brought about the trivialization of nature, the banalization of all thought processes. If death is the final mineralization of all living matter, we are as a civilization not far from this state. And yet, I should dare this apophthegm: *There is nothing trivial in nature.* If science had really remained the search for truth about nature, I should have extended my statement to say

---

*Lucan's beautiful hexameter had made a deep impression on me when I was young: *Victrix causa deis placuit, sed victa Catoni.* Cato could in our time hardly have qualified for a research grant; it would all have gone to the gods.

that there is nothing trivial in science. But we all know how untrue this would be if we are to debit, as we must, science with all the twaddle it has generated. (One of my devils, in charge of banalities, whispers into my ear: "Why don't you say, there is science and science?" Well, I shall not say it; there is only one kind of science, but we seldom practice it.)

Our thoughts about nature may be trivial, because we are trivial thinkers, and so may be our explanations of the experimental observations; but how about a fact, can it be trivial? Here I seem to be in trouble, for I have often complained about the excessive number of papers of the utmost banality being published at an increasing rate, each full of so-called facts of nature, bringing us news that nobody cares to hear. This is unquestionably true, for until recently, when the vultures of insolvency began to peep through the windows of the laboratories, money was more easily had than ideas, although the decision on what to observe and the ability to interpret what one had seen could not be bought for any sum. At that time we got the good together with the bad, a little of the first, much of the latter, approximately in human proportions. The difficulty began when money vanished, for now a very hard choice had to be made and predestination had to operate even before conception. The celebrated Juvenalian question, namely, who should watch the watchers, suddenly became pertinent; and the sad answer was that were was nobody suitable around. Even the pigs must be trained to find the truffles; but few of us have been taught to discern the light when it is hidden under an unmarked bushel. At this moment the nefarious influence of scientific fashions began to be felt; a distortion about which I shall soon say a few words.

There exist, however, scientific observations that reveal facts relevant to the understanding of nature; facts that cannot be trivial and experiments leading to their uncovering which cannot be trivial. Only a time that, in its cocksure conceit, sees little value in verifying generally accepted models or dogmas could have condemned experiments that had not been done before as trivial. These people would obviously have preferred bivial or even univial experiments. I believe, I should have been better understood 100 or 150 years ago, which shows how unenlightened the founders of our sciences were. On the other hand, G. E. Stahl had he still been alive, would certainly have given a low "priority" to Lavoisier.

V

What is it that produces, subconsciously for most of us, a ranking among the compounds and the systems of living nature? And what makes most scientists choose one field of study rather than another? The second question invites a cynical answer: they swim in schools and go where the food is plentiful. But I believe, although the economic view of research has much to recommend itself, that this would be an oversimplification. It is in dark caverns of the human mind that there arises the curse of fashions, encoded no doubt in unknown regions of the DNA which cannot yet be explored since no messenger RNA for miniskirts has been discovered.

The fashions of science? They exist, but they seem to come from nowhere and they disappear again, and nobody can say why or even when. This is true of all fashions, although a study of changing garment styles will not enlighten us very much about what may really be periodic variations attendant upon a profound Heraclitean principle of eternal change. In any event, when I tried to inform myself through a study of various treatises, such as the book of Roland Barthes,[3] I came away not wiser, but more somnolent. The changing fashions of science are rather comparable to the changes in literary, musical or artistic taste that characterize different periods. Why did Goethe admire the paintings of Guercino or Guido Reni, whereas now they seldom leave the storage rooms of the museums? What are the reasons of the past neglect and current revival of baroque literature and music? No doubt there exist people who could explain all this to me, but I should not understand them in spite of all their semiology and the search for the "signifier" and the "signified" and even the "paradigm." I might as well try to get an answer by interviewing

King Aiolos, the Master of the Winds; but he is rather un-
communicative, as Odysseus found out on his second visit.
It would unquestionably be of great interest to follow the
onset, the climax, and the decline of such concepts as "hard
porn" or "viral oncology"—to take two very different ema-
nations of our sloganified century—and to determine
whether they follow recognizable laws. Even this would not
help us very much, except for telling us how long these notions last. As for scientific fashions I should think that they
last longer than women's fashions but not as long as men's.

VI

When I got into biochemistry, many years ago, intermediary metabolism and vitamins or coenzymes were the great
thing; so I worked on carotinoids, structural lipids and lipo-
proteins, polysaccharides, and blood coagulation. Then the
proteins and later the enzymes moved to the center; but I
worked on inositol, hydroxy amino acids, and then on nucleic acids. When the nucleic acids took over with a tremendous wallop, I moved to enzymes, mostly of a modest nature. Now that the nucleic acids have nearly spent their
aroma, I expect that membranes are the thing to watch—
and so it goes. At one period or another, I seem to have
touched upon almost everything, but always at the wrong
time.

This sorry-go-round of human vanities could be completed by similarly sketching the rise, decline and fall of the
various status symbols of the laboratory scientist, the color-
imeters, spectrophotometers, NMR machines, mass spec-
trographs, ultracentrifuges, scintillation counters, computers, etc., always moving by $5000-jumps into the
stratosphere of complete financial and intellectual bank-
ruptcy in which we find ourselves today.

Another particularly silly aspect of this vanity fair is the
continuous alternation of permissible research objects. At
one time you could get money only for work on animal
organs; bacteria were out. Then suddenly bacteria were in,
everything else was taboo. A little later, all this changed
again. Bacteriophage workers, once the kings of the coven,

now populate the debtors' prisons. Procaryotes are proscribed, eucaryotes acclaimed. Animal viruses, long an object of suspicion, commiseration, and neglect, are highly quoted and oversubscribed. The Oscars of science do not set trends, but follow them. Had Peyton Rous not lived to be eighty-seven, he would not have been honored. (With Leo Tolstoy, on the other hand, dead at only eighty-two, all hope was buried in an early grave.)

VII

Mentioning the bizarre oscillations of scientific fashions made me look a little more closely at the entire problem of fashion; I came to the conclusion that we are dealing with two waves, one of a very large amplitude and spread, superimposed on a whole series of lesser ones. The large wave I should better call "style," and it may embrace an entire century or an even longer period. The origins of the style of an era are completely mysterious to me. Is style a minute reflection, as it were, of the systole and diastole of the universe? Is it by rhythmic changes that the world breathes, that it stays alive? I do not believe that any man or group of men can influence this gigantic movement. The tiny ripples under the great wave—we could call them "fashions" or "vogue" or, in some cases, even "taste"—are, however, certainly promoted or even produced by what our publicity-drunk time would designate as tastemakers, trend-setters, etc. These cardboard celebrities then make up the establishments of the various branches of human endeavor, be it hot rock or geophysics. If I were to use the comparison with our taste in music that I have drawn before, I should say that the relative popularity of baroque music is somehow connected with the style of our time and, hence, beyond the control of the individual, but that the enormous number of works by, say, Vivaldi or Telemann being played now is due to the efforts of the recording industry.

If I am correct in what I just said, it is the style of a period that conditions, or even compels, us to accept and adopt its various fashions or fads. As concerns the natural sciences, and especially biology, one could perhaps say that the trend

to an extreme form of primitive reductionism is a facet of
the style of our epoch, whereas the various fluctuations in
centers of attention and acclaim of which I have spoken
before correspond to the micro-ripples under the great
wave. One after the other of the so-called mysteries of nature are being explained away until the time when a new
wave takes over, giving rise to a new set of equally evanescent explanations. If I were entrusted with seeking out the
wave of the future, I would assemble a committee of experts, guaranteed to be very dim-witted; and if they advised me strongly against doing something, this I would
do.

A true appreciation of the validity of quality judgments
will, therefore, require a knowledge of the quality of the
judges, for a committee of camels will never approve a
horse. It would be safer to leave the decision to a tombola.
The old German proverb *Wem Gott ein Amt gibt, dem gibt er
auch Verstand* is no longer true. This may have been so
when God distributed the offices and duties; but in the
meantime much more mundane, and hence more immund,
mechanisms have been operating.

Decisions on science policy—regardless of whether we
deal with the huge sums spent on the sinister campaign to
wipe out cancer* or with the small grants to individual in-
vestigators—are made with an eye on what is quoted most
highly on the stock market of permissible science. They are
made under the sway of the rapidly changing fashions of
which I have spoken before. Entire scientific disciplines
with a great tradition may be eliminated, as for instance
botany is in the course of being now; and if a country is

---

*I do not, of course, object to the attempt to overcome one of the
scourges of mankind—to make room no doubt for another one—
only to the way in which we go about it. But is it not remarkable
that, as by one command, every other university, institute of technology, and research laboratory feels the sudden need of opening a
cancer institute? One must be astonished at the sudden plethora of
therapeutic talent, though not without fear of the coming day of
reckoning.

overtaken by spiritual elephantiasis it will see to it that the individual scientist—working in his small laboratory, facing every night his own consciousness, his own responsibility—is replaced by huge phalansteries in which the production, by the ton, of predictable pseudo-discoveries is more efficient in terms of cost accounting. In the eyes of the efficiency experts small science must appear as trivial science.

Having thus closed the circle, I may return to the starting point. What, then, is a trivial enzyme?

VIII

In hell everything has its price. When the new building of the Infernal Bureau of Investigation was inaugurated, the headlines were: "126 Million IBI Building Opens in Erebus." And when the Devil went to somebody's house, the newspaper said: "Beelzebub Visits 250,000 Country Home." (Not knowing the currency unit, I have omitted it.)

Similarly, we are wont to assume, perhaps conditioned by our violent age, that nature is a heavyweight brute. Mindless wasters of energy, as we are, we should like to sprinkle ATP on everything. Whether we believe in an expanding, contracting, or stationary universe, we should like it to be a violent universe. What earlier centuries considered as a divine and gentle force has become for us a perpetual explosion of uncounted megatons. We subject living nature to an incessant "overkill," as if we were dealing with a larger and even more recalcitrant Vietnam. There must appear to us something wrong in Pascal's *silence éternel des espaces infinis,* in the silence of the universe.

This violence-tinged vision of nature is also being transferred to our speculations on the living cell which, even if it is not depicted as a steaming powerhouse, we like to see engage in reactions consuming a lot of energy. If the cell possesses, for instance, an enzyme that can perform a certain reaction at an expense of seven kilocalories, then why bother with a 2-kcal-enzyme that does similar things? We shall consider the latter as a trivial, an unimportant enzyme;

and anyone wanting to work on it will be penalized by not getting money.

In speaking of enzymes, I may mention that they have themselves become the victims of one of the abrupt turn-abouts in scientific fashions to which I have alluded before. It is, I believe, not an exaggeration to say that the study of the chemistry and of the reaction mechanisms of many enzymes has been one of the greatest triumphs of biochemistry in the recent past. But as more of these proteins have been purified to homogeneity, as their chemical structure has been elucidated, as their mode of action has been defined, they have been converted into objects of chemistry rather than of biology; they have changed sciences, as it were, and have at the same time somehow fallen out of fashion.

This has to do with what I once called "the paradox of biochemistry," namely, that biochemistry is helpless before life, having to kill the organism before investigating it. Biochemistry is, in fact, much more successful in practicing the second part of its composite name than in following the prefix. Statements of this sort should, but usually do not, elicit the question, "What is meant by success in science?" In our context the answer is not difficult: fulfilling, as completely as possible, the expectations of the particular fashion. For instance, in our time a successful cancer researcher is not one who "solves the riddle," but rather one who gets a lot of money to do so. It is all quite similar to the history of alchemy, another truly goal-directed, though much less costly, enterprise. Unfortunately, the greedy old kings who sponsored those ancient researchers occasionally proved quite resentful of failure.

I conclude, hence, that triviality is what the fashions abhor. It is, however, evident that the way to the pantheon of the bitch goddesses whose name is success, is paved with erstwhile trivialities that have outlived or overcome their proscription.

8.
VOICES IN THE LABYRINTH
Dialogues Around the Study of Nature

Amphisbaena

. . . *et tu in te manes,*
nos autem in experimentis volvimur? [1]
Augustinus, *Confessiones*, IV, 5

'Tis all in peeces, all cohaerance gone;
All just supply, and all Relation.
Donne, "An Anatomie of the World,"
The First Anniversary, lines 213–14

Nay, so devoted are we to this principle,
and at the same time so curiously mechanical, that a new trade, specially
grounded on it, has arisen among us,
under the name of "Codification," or
code-making in the abstract; whereby
any people, for a reasonable consideration, may be accommodated with a patent code;—more easily than curious individuals with patent breeches, for the
people does not need to be measured
first.
Carlyle, *Signs of the Times* (1829)

It is August, 1961. Two men—an Old Chemist, O, and a Young Molecular Biologist, Y—sit on a bench.

O: Now that I have you here for a few minutes of quiet talk, I shall start by saying: The cell is not a machine.

Y: But what kind of a start would that be? Do you want me to agree? This would surely be stupid, for there are all sorts of machines, and you have probably never heard of the theory of automata. I should much rather turn your statement around and say: A machine is a cell.

O: We are then already in the middle of model-building, the favorite occupation of modern biophysics. It is all done in front of mirrors, with wire and plastic, glue and papier-mâché; the knowledge of a child combined with the naïveté of the grown-up.

Y: But really, why are you so against machines?

O: Of course I am not; some of my best friends are machines. But I am very much against a strictly mechanomorphic view of living nature. A machine is a deterministic construction; someone—an intelligence—has had to make it; and even if it could be "programmed" to make itself, who did the programming? A self-reproducing machine that was not built by a primordial engineer is an abomination thrown up by turbulent and sick times which, in chiliastic dreams mixing superpower and impotence, have created a mythology of a most maculate conception. I shall not formulate the secret of life sitting on this bench on a summer day; but I can say that we shall not have a satisfactory theory of biology before we have learned to combine, in one concept, the dialectic play between determinism and accident—a sort of random nonrandomness—which seems to characterize the living and reproducing cell.

Y: It would seem to me that you are simply an angry old man preaching some sort of dialectical biochemistry in which the observer is walking simultaneously on both sides of the street in opposite directions. One could call this also schizophrenic.

O: Well, as to being an angry old man, there is plenty to be angry about, and it makes more sense for an old man to be angry than for a young one; like most things, anger must be earned. King Lear was an angry old man. We are no longer accustomed to passion in the natural sciences; it has been replaced by ambition. Our young geniuses are passionately ambitious instead of being passionately passionate; and it has become very difficult to distinguish between what is an ardent search for truth and what is a vigorous promotion campaign. What started as an adventure of the highest has become the survival of the slickest or the quickest. "Cloak and dagger" has changed to "cloak and suit." We now have DNA tycoons and others have "made a killing" in RNA. A generation of scientific quiz kids knowing the answer to everything. But to throw pearls before young molecular biologists is not the purpose of this talk. Let's return to the beginning and I will ask you: "What is molecular biology?" Now, if physics is the science of the states, chemistry that of the conversions of matter, and biology comprises the application of their laws to animate nature, what could be meant by molecular biology? You can, of course, apply any adjective to any noun, but the results are most often bizarre.

Y: Here you go again. I could, of course, be witty, as you think you are, and say that molecular biology is what is published in the journal carrying that name. All academic gowns carry, strictly speaking, the color of their respective payrolls.

O: Here I interrupt already. Your jocular definition cannot hold, since the irregular rate of appearance of this admirable journal is vastly inferior to that at which molecular biologists are produced nowadays. My definition, incidentally, would be that molecular biology is essentially the practice of biochemistry without a license.

Y: This is, as you must know, a completely frivolous definition. There is naturally much more to molecular biology. In order to prevent you from going on endlessly, I shall agree that the naming of a new science—or a new name for an old one—also has its practical reasons. Symposia, congresses, new journals, more money to be had more easily . . .

O: And the feeling to be a pioneer at no extra cost. And how the publishers love these new handles by which to extract the old money. In fact, this is not the end; soon we shall have molecular sociology, molecular history, and a little later perhaps molecular theology. The fragmentation of the sciences proceeds via adjectives.

Y: I believe that even among your age group, you are a horrible exception.

O: Very likely. In a time in which everything that is new is true, the older the fogy the more he must galvanize himself into being able to participate in the exuberant initiation dances that greet each new molecule before it is replaced by an even newer one. But I must say, you can't escape senility by trying to become a juvenile delinquent.

Y: I shall ignore this. What I said a moment ago about the advantages of having a new science was not meant satirically. This is the way sciences grow in our day; they have become a mass movement, a corporation in which the majority of the population carry stock. Their development must be studied by the methods of sociology.

O: Another stew of a science.

Y: Let's slaughter one at a time. To return to our subject—if we still have one—this is, I believe, the way our new science came about. It started with the recognition of the importance of macromolecules in biology, of their chemically distinct and precisely describable structures, and of the specific functions which very often could be clearly assigned to them. Take the enzymes . . .

O: I will take them. But who did the assigning? You isolate a protein, you ask it a very limited number of questions by bringing it together with a few substances. If it happens to react with one or the other, you call them "substrates" and you proceed to assign a specific function to this particular protein. Did you notice the man that passed us a moment ago? He limped; and you would rightly say that this was because he had one leg shorter than the other. But how could I refute someone who claimed that this man had one leg too short in order to limp? You say that this enzyme is present in the cell, in order to perform this reaction. *Hic Rhodus, hic salta!* But maybe this is not Rhodes or maybe he does not jump, or maybe he jumps somewhere else. For instance, let us assume you have some sort of cell mush and you fish out several enzymes that all seem to do the same thing in the test tube. How sure can you be that they all really act this way in the living cell, that this is their "function"? Ours—and yours—still is a *post mortem* science; we are forced to destroy the overriding, the overpowering category of life.

Y: Don't tell me you are a vitalist.

O: Of course not. But a discussion between us about the meaning of life would be stupid: I am too rigid and you are too flexible. All I can say is, life is what's lost in the test tube. Better tell me your opinion about what I said concerning the assigning of functions.

Y: I think there are such enzymes and such. Many have the functions that we have given them, others may not be called upon to act under normal circumstances; they may be a memory that the cell has retained of past events. But surely even you cannot deny that, for instance, the energy relationships of the cell and their enzymic basis are well understood and are the best example of the concept of the unity of biochemistry.

O: This I will not deny, thought I cannot say that I am particularly fond of this concept of unity. It has done a lot of mischief. Life, as we know it, seems to be characterized by two antithetical principles: unity and diversity. And it is very difficult to decide, in a concrete case, with which of these principles we are dealing. The unity of nature is usually laboriously pieced together by combining, in a spuriously serial or cyclic fashion, snips and bits taken from the most widely distant organisms. It is a sort of biomontage or biocollage. The fact that we all live and die in one and the same world should not conceal another fact: that we are all different. Even life is only one, and a minor, form of nature: a tiny foam on the crystals of the earth. For an old man who is in love with what goes on around him and with the multiformity of its appearances there can be only one battle cry: *Vive la différence!* Is it really so important that both torturer and victim enjoyed the same hearty meal and digested it in the same manner? Besides, similar mechanisms do not always foreshadow similar functions. The combustion oven designed by Liebig and the combustion ovens constructed in Auschwitz, though based on the same scientific principles, can hardly be taken as a proof of the unity of nature. But your little speech about the processes of parturition that resulted in the forceps delivery of molecular biology stopped at the enzymes. Perhaps you go on.

Y: What you like to call my little speech did not stop, it was stopped. In any event, the recognition that polypeptides of high molecular weight could show great specificity as enzymes in metabolic reactions and as antigens or antibodies in immunology led to many studies of their physical and chemical structures. Ultracentrifugation, X-ray diffraction, electrophoresis, electron microscopy, and the many wonderful separation methods carrying the name of chromatography were all instrumental in bringing about these exciting times. It became possible not only to analyze proteins completely but even to determine their amino acid sequence in many cases. The triumphs of structure determination were so great that everywhere young people were flocking to the banner of the helical nature of things.

O: You are spiraling a little too fast for me. Even Lucretius had to stop for breath. Your dithyrambic tone reminds me that not long ago I heard a gushing voice on the radio speaking of "DNA, this miracle monocule."

Y: What of it? Some people have difficulty pronouncing the word *molecule;* but this will change. Just as there were times when people found it easy to say *transubstantiation.* As for

DNA, I shall soon come to it. Let me continue. The advances I mentioned a minute ago were, of course, not the only ones. Even before they had come to fruition, studies had begun on other fronts. Certain viruses had been purified sufficiently so as to warrant their chemical examination and had been recognized as nucleoproteins. First came the plant viruses which were found to contain RNA, as do most of the animal viruses. The bacteriophages, on the other hand, contain mostly DNA. But perhaps the most exciting thing that happened—now I can admit it since the old man who did it is dead—was the discovery that microbial transformation, a phenomenon known for quite some time, was due to specific forms of DNA. This had the effect of placing DNA very near to what the geneticists at that time were still calling the gene.

O: If you don't mind, let us stick to this hoary term. I know that the packaging has been changed lately; but, since it still is the same old thing, why not conserve the convenient brand name? After all, if you want to describe a syndrome you must first give it a name. The one advantage, for instance, that I can see in using the term "molecular biology" is that it puts nearly all that is unknown in biochemistry into one convenient corner. But I wanted to say a word about transforming DNA. I well remember the great excitement with which I followed the first discoveries concerning specific pneumococcal deoxyribonucleic acid. Then we still spoke of "desoxyribonucleic." In fact, this was probably the main reason for my becoming interested in the nucleic acids at about that time—1944 or 1945. But it has been a long time since then and not so very much has happened in this field; I must confess that my misgivings about the justification of expanding these few observations on microorganisms to the entire realm of life have been growing at an ever-increasing rate. Generalization has its definite uses in science; without it, all of us would soon be without jobs. But at the same time, there is a great danger of its sliding into glibness. It was in 1889 that the great Swiss historian Jacob Burckhardt wrote a letter to a friend in which he warned of the oncoming of what he called *les terribles simplificateurs.* Just as the locusts, once they are through with a field, have simplified it horribly, could we not say that this is also true of some of the great generalizations in biology? Color and variety, the pulsations of accident and fate, the tremendous urges and instincts, the pendulum of birth and death—all have disappeared and we are left with what I once called "a plantation of matchsticks." So, when I listen to the arguments that microbial transformation proves the gene character of DNA, I must ask if this discovery is one of the features of the unity of nature or one of the facets of its diversity. That's where the dialectics which we referred at the beginning of our little disputation comes in.

Y: I can see that you want to keep your cake and sell it too. You are an intolerable mystic; I have had the feeling that, while you speak of nature, there should be a slight music of harps. Why do you keep plucking the feathers out of the goose that lays golden eggs for all of us? After all, you are one of the classics in this field.

O: Thank you, but I would rather not be. According to your definition, a classic in science is a man who no longer has to be quoted. For the pickpocket, the man with the widest pockets is a classic. And it has been remarked that Banquo is seldom quoted in Macbeth's papers.

Y: All right, then I shall call you a Cassandra in long pants. But my story was not yet entirely finished. I had been talking about transforming DNA; and if you had not broken in I should have continued by mentioning other instances in which nucleic acids were assigned direct roles in the determination of hereditary properties. For instance, there are the bacteriophages attacking *E. coli* which seem to do it by injecting their specific DNA into the bacterial cell. This is enough to set off an entire chain of events terminating in the production of many phage particles and the rupture of the host cell. And then we have the plant viruses; they contain specific types of RNA which are infective; that means that the nucleic acid itself, when applied to the plant, can give rise to the formation of innumerable complete virus particles. These are all definite and specific molecules exerting definite and specific biological effects; and here you have the quintessence of our new science: molecular biology. But this is not all.

O: I am sure it is not. Even to sell soap nowadays, you need an *a cappella* choir. What baffles an old-fashioned chemist about all this is what has become of the chemical concept of a molecule. I have heard people of a still older generation claim that this concept ends with the applicability of Avogadro's law. But never mind. In any event, it must have been a pleasant surprise for some biologists to learn that at last they were dealing with molecules. I should have thought that this was what they had been doing all the time. It reminds me a bit of Monsieur Jourdain in Molière's *Bourgeois Gentilhomme* who is astonished to hear that what he has been speaking all his life is called "prose."

Y: Surely you must have heard the term "molecular disease?"

O: Alas, I have; and for a time I thought that this was a disease to which molecules were particularly prone, a sort of molecular measles. But I soon learned that this was another symptom of the general sloganification of science, everything—like in a poor cartoon—having a pithy label hanging from the mouth. Some of these slogans may have been convenient or useful at one time, such as "energy-rich phosphate bonds," "dynamic state of body constituents"; of others I am less sure. But there are so many of them, and they are so glittering, so glib! The more I hear them, the less I enjoy them. The peculiar relationship between names and understanding has often been discussed, best perhaps by Mephistopheles.

Y: Great concepts require great names.

O: Or perhaps great names can substitute for great concepts. But I believe that you had not yet finished.

Y: This is correct, for I now have to introduce the crowning concept, namely, "biological information."

O: Do you mean to say that life itself has now acquired a press agent?

Y: Of course not; but there has arisen all over the world a group of young, militant and successful practitioners— evangelists, you might call them—who are spreading the new knowledge with devotion and perseverance. All seems to fit.

O: Or at least you disregard what doesn't. Such must have been the atmosphere when Phlogiston went strong, all seemed to fit until a little balance was brought into play. Even the great Ockham with his immortal razor would no longer succeed in shaving the multicolored beard that is now sprouting all over the beautiful face of biochemistry. Opening one issue of a journal, I am assailed by an abysmal cackle of terms, ill-fitting, yet strident, garish and banal. The shockate, the grindate and the sonicate, the suicide and the abortion, the fingerprints and the hot spots, the repressors and the co-repressors, the feedbacks, the pools and the templates, the regulators, the operators and the operons; and floating over the entire allegorical cesspool, the mysterious messengers, angelic and diabolic in their evanescent everywhereness. Have we really arrived at the stage of non-objective biochemistry, of molecular action painting?

Y: You have left out the hybrids and many other things; but I am glad to see that you are fairly familiar with our nomenclature. Let me say, however, that to make a scientific revolution one must break many eggheads. Your objections are ineffective and they will not count in the end. Biological or, if you prefer, genetic information is an extremely important and useful concept which even a Shakespearean fool cannot laugh off. Before I go on I should like to ask you a question. When trying to understand the life of the cell and the functions of its individual parts, don't you believe in the division of labor?

O: Frankly, I don't; at least not in the crudely mechanomorphic way—the wheels and the gears and the levers—in which this is usually done. Even if nature were one gigantic servo-mechanism, I am afraid the beards of the cyberneticists, entrusted with servicing it, would get in the way of the feedbacks. In the living cell there must be a way in which quantity—or, better, density or compression—regulated on an as yet undescribable time scale, becomes a new and unique quality, namely, that of life.

Y: I am afraid, you are, after all, a vitalist. Returning now to this business of information and disregarding all you have said, this is what it amounts to. We do believe in the division of labor in the cell, with each part, yes, with each molecule, having a definite and recognizable function. And we believe in the existence of a strict hierarchy.

O: I know, I know. Mix anything with everything in the right proportions and the resulting purée will say "Papa!" But tell me, since you mention the hierarchy of the cell, reading the recent literature I get the impression that the cell is a society of slaves that has no master.

Y: Not at all. In the beginning was DNA . . .

O: I hear the start of a new apocryphal gospel with DNA as the logos of our times.

Y: Is it possible that you don't believe in DNA?

O: If I don't believe that the moon is made of green cheese, does this necessarily mean that I don't believe in the moon?

Y: Anyway, DNA is the genetic material which in the last resort is responsible for the maintenance and the transmission of the hereditary properties of the cell. We know about the mechanism of its replication which is an ingenious deduction from the generally accepted structural model of DNA: a double helix composed of two intertwined polynucleotide chains. After the separation of these strands—which is very easy to explain, as it offers no thermodynamic difficulties and can be carried out with a model costing less than a dollar—each strand now proceeds to the production of its counterpart.

O: How general is general? And without wanting to offend your sense of economy, thermodynamical or otherwise, may I ask whether you mean that this beautiful scheme applies to meiosis as well as mitosis?

Y: I am not interested in diploids.

O: I wish your parents had felt the same way. And would you say that during the splitting of a chromosome the other constituents—the proteins, the lipids—undergo similar processes? Or do they simply follow the leader out of family affection?

Y: Let's not waste our time with trivialities. Who cares about lipids anyway? The smart cookies leave them alone. I shall give you a purely formal scheme which you can take or leave; but you would be well advised to take it.

O: Scientific dogmas are phagocytes which eat only what is good for them. They cannot be refuted or dethroned; but they vanish eventually owing to the fickleness of subsequent generations who lose interest in them. In fact, the more absurd a hypothesis is, the stronger must be the belief in it.

Y: To continue, DNA is the primary genetic determinant carrying a code through which, in the last resort, the composition of RNA and the proteins is specified. Before this code can be expressed, the two strands composing the double helix of the DNA must be separated, unwound, perhaps enzymatically. I believe it was you who called this hypothetical enzyme an "unscrewase." You will observe that, because of the complementary structure of the two strands, the information stored in either one really is sufficient.

O: Have the two strands been shown to exist, let alone to have a complementary structure?

Y: Well, yes and no. But you should be the last to ask such a question.

O: Sometimes I wake up in the dark of the night and I begin to think of all these claims and discoveries and models, of all this molecular prestidigitation; and I ask myself: If this is all a confidence game. They are all so brilliant; why are they so shallow? Why did the manna of the heavens turn into porridge? Why does the liquidation of a science begin at the top; why do its greatest triumphs turn into its worst disasters?

Y: I don't believe you expect an answer. All you have to do is to take a spectra of a DNA before and after heating.

O: Now I can see that you are a modern young scientist. Is not the use of these false singulars—a spectra, a media, a bacteria, a phenomena or even a phenomenum, etc.—the *summa cum laude* of the new generation?

Y: I have never found Latin useful in my work. If you, too, had studied more mathematics and physics, instead of wasting your time, you would have accomplished more.

O: This may very well be so. I have felt for some time that your Ph.D. should be spelled pH D.

Y: In any event, this is how it works. There is no doubt at all, the direction is DNA to RNA to protein; but never backwards. The genetic signals emanating from the DNA go first to a special kind of RNA which turns over very rapidly, never amounts to more than a few percent of the total RNA of the cell, and mimics, in its composition, that of the DNA. Since it carries the message contained in the DNA, we call it the messenger RNA.

O: This small and short-lived Corps of Commissionnaires, has anyone seen it?

Y: What do you mean by "seen it"? There is plenty of indirect evidence that such an RNA is formed.

O: No, I mean the message, has anyone shown that it exists? Is it not possible that the entire imposing terminological scaffold is nothing but a suitcase for the emperor's new clothes? Is it not possible that there is no message, no messenger, that the entire question is asked, and therefore answered, wrongly?

Y: If you deny that there is such a thing as "information," you will still have to get the same fellow, but call him by a different name.

O: You want to say what is usually said when one has no answer, that this is merely semantics?

Y: Yes. Incidentally, messenger RNA is not the only name; others have referred to it as informational RNA or pulse RNA. The men that really discovered the stuff gave it no name and will therefore be rightly forgotten.

O: This is true; never be a pioneer. Those who come first in science do not count; only those who come last. But let us stay with these charming conceits for a little while and try to think things through. I know that today what cannot be done indirectly isn't being done at all. But chemistry is, after all, the science of substances; and if all this is true there must be a substantial basis to it. You said that it all starts with DNA. This DNA, I take it, exists in the cell as a double-stranded helix, as what people with a brilliant gift for vulgarization have called "the coil of life." The two strands run in opposite directions with respect to their terminal phosphates and have a complementary nucleotide sequence, so that purines can pair with pyrimidines, adenine with thymine, and guanine with cytosine. And you might say that this scheme was confirmed before it was devised, since this had been shown to be true of the composition of DNA. It has been forgotten completely that the specific base-pairing in nucleic acids was discovered in an old-fashioned chemical laboratory.

Y: Well, I happen to remember, but who cares? What did these people whom you call old fashioned do to make their findings known?

O: They published them.

Y: Published? Are you being jocular? Is this what you call aggressive scholarship? Did they send out mimeographed copies of their papers long before publication? Did they found base-pairing clubs? Did they distribute neckties with suitable emblems?

O: But who would want to spend his life dancing a minuet before assembled science reporters? There are still people who do not wish to join the noise boys; they have other concerns. When you start on something new you are all alone and it is so terribly dark; and then, suddenly, you come face to face with the blinding whiteness of reality. There is nothing more exquisite, nothing rarer in the world. Afterwards you have a choice: you stay in the laboratory, hoping that it will happen again—it seldom does—or you begin to travel through the country giving minstrel shows.

Y: Anyway, even if the composition of DNA had been found entirely different, we should have doubted the analysis rather than our concept.

O: I can see, you are a True Believer. It is with such deductions that the road to the paradise of scientists is paved. But really, I did not wish to attack what one is pleased to call the "central dogma," for I know that the mythopoeic urge of humanity does not stop at the door of the laboratory. But let me continue and I shall assume that the existence of two complementary strands, each having two ends, a head and a tail, as it were, has been proved.

Y: Well, if it hasn't, it will be.

O: This DNA, as I understand it, has two functions. It has to make itself—that is easy: unscrew, assemble, polymerize, recombine. This has now become a so-called project for the so-called science fairs of our so-called high school boys. But it also has to make the rest of the cell; and this is not so easy. For in this DNA must be contained the quintessence of all this tremendous life of our earth, the flagellum and the spirillum, but also the brain that invented the St. Matthew Passion. *Dinanzi a me non fuor cose create . . .*[2]

Y: Don't talk Latin at me.

O: Never mind. What I wanted to point out is that nowadays DNA plays the role of a self-replicating philosopher's stone. First we have an extremely vicious circle: DNA makes DNA makes DNA, etc.; a dreary, tragic desert, an Yves Tanguy landscape. But simultaneously—and by what delegation of functions even you could not tell me—the Dr.

Jekyll side of DNA gets into the act and makes *A* and *B* and *C*. I am always being told that all biological information resides, in the last resort, in DNA. But organisms contain many types of specific molecules, quite apart from the proteins and the nucleic acids: the mysterious conjugated proteins, some of the lipids, cell wall substances, antibodies, blood group substances, specific polysaccharides.

Y: These polysaccharides contain no information.

O: How do you know? Did you talk with them lately? But let me return to our argument. When DNA gives play to the friendlier part of its nature, the first thing it does, I am told, is to preside over the manufacture of messenger RNA. This RNA is said to show the composition regularities of the entire DNA. If the latter really consists of two complementary strands, this must mean that two complementary RNA strands, or a mixture of shorter pieces amounting in the aggregate to two such strands, have been made. To put it more concretely, a triple uracil in one messenger polynucleotide would have to correspond to a triple adenine in the complementary RNA structure. Since a ribosome—"they also serve who only stand and wait"—can make a protein only when it is "programmed" by a messenger RNA which on the whole cannot be a double strand, as it must be able to engage in specific hydrogen-bonding, the conclusion would have to be that any given section of a DNA dyad should give rise to two entirely different proteins. Would you consequently subscribe to the revised slogan "one gene, two enzymes"?

Y: Well, I don't know. There are a hundred ways out.

O: But should a scientist behave like a tracked cockroach? I know that almost anything you can write on a piece of paper will eventually be realized in a so-called system and then it will form a "fact." I cannot help feeling, however, that not all facts are equally worth knowing. I thought it was the task of the natural sciences to discover the facts of nature, not to create them.

Y: You are just an obscurantist.

O: I have often been accused of spreading darkness. And I cannot deny that the dazzling light being thrown on a few spots to the exclusion of the rest has distorted all the proportions of our science. How many frantic about-faces someone of my age has had to live through! And the yelping is not at an end; in fact, it is getting worse. Miss Molecule of 1962 remains to be crowned; and I fear—and you hope—there will be many more. The next candidate will no doubt be messenger RNA. But to continue with what I was saying before. You may, of course, ascribe to my advancing years the difficulties I experience in understanding what is claimed to go on. Even if we accept the existence of a short-lived species of RNA that is made under the direct control of DNA and by mirroring the composition of the latter transfers the information from DNA to the proteins, and if we add the relatively small amount of so-called soluble RNA, we are left with the bulk, almost eighty-five percent, of the cellular RNA for which neither function nor mode of formation is apparent. You will, of course, with your usual originality tell me that Rome was not built in a day, to which I shall reply that less credit should be given to those who fail to solve great problems than to those that succeed in solving small ones. There is nothing easier than to fall off Mount Everest.

Y: Well, first you have to get there. But you cannot deny the existence of a rapidly turning-over RNA that does mirror the composition of DNA, in base-pairing, etc.

O: Most of the analyses that I have seen are far from convincing. A lot of good will or, better, lack of experience is necessary for such enthusiastically sweeping claims. But never mind, many people have made a good living in science by selling the emperor's new clothes. *De nihilo nihil* does not hold for molecular biology. Only where there is nothing, all is possible. If you consider a cell, and the amount of packing or compression it must require, the traffic problems become so enormous as to demand the formulation of a new dimension for which we lack even the slightest intimation; instead of which we are being fed terminological cant. DNA slowly reproducing itself and at the same time rushing to make hundreds of different messengers; all these messengers milling about madly in search of ribosomal easy chairs on which to procreate and die; proteins peeling off and proceeding to their respective posts; unborn lipids and polysaccharides crying for nonexistant templates: a molecular Walpurgisnacht, a federation meeting of the universe, only even less comfortable than in Atlantic City. It would all be very funny if it did not corrupt our youth. Who, when he knew it when it was *so* small, would have thought of DNA as the demiurgos of a Manichaean world?

Y: You are using too many long words to say nothing. The fact that you knew DNA when it had a molecular weight of 800,000, whereas now it is up to 160 million, is of no significance, except to show that you did not know how to invest wisely.

O: Of course this is not at all that I meant. But even if we reconcile ourselves to this bizarre situation and accept the notion that everything that happens in a cell is under the ultimate control of DNA, we encounter other difficulties. Many viruses are essentially ribonucleoproteins; and in several cases their RNA itself has been shown to be infective. You mentioned it yourself before. This RNA is presumably able to replicate itself; but where is the specific DNA that presides over this replication?

Y: I can give you two different answers. I could assume that there is something special about viral RNA that enables it to act as its own template, independently of any control exercised by DNA.

O: But this is a self-strangling argument. Shouldn't viral RNA show complete base-pairing in this case? Besides, from the chemical point of view, there does not seem to be anything special about the RNA of viruses. Incidentally, since in this reasoning all roles are reversed, I expect to hear almost any day about a "messenger DNA."

Y: I have an alternative answer. Let us assume that all RNA, viral as well as ribosomal, transfer or messenger, is made under the control of DNA, but only in the case of messenger are both DNA strands involved; the other RNA species reflect the composition of a single strand of DNA. By now you must credit me with enough intelligence to propose hundred plausible schemes to explain this.

O: I would not go so far; but for n problems you will always have $n + 1$ mutually exclusive, but equally irrefutable, explanations.

Y: Never mind. So far as virus RNA is concerned, a second assumption must, of course, be made: for a cell to be able to support a certain virus it must contain, as part of its genome, a stretch of DNA that is normally nonoperative, but becomes active under the influence of the invading viral RNA molecule. It is this DNA portion that is reflected by the infective RNA.

O: I feel like Peer Gynt in the cave of the trolls, refusing to undergo a simple eye operation that would permit him to see straight what looks crooked to him. You, too, will undoubtedly grow into one of our synthetic geniuses—these fake celebrities, glued together with the spittle of Madison Avenue—of whom there are so many that they clutter up the place. And yet the combined brainpower of all these cytopractors would not fill the inkwell of Pascal. To them, everything is so simple. The hypnotic effect of repeating nonsensical statements over and over has produced a general trance that is mistaken for a view of nature. I was taught that it is the task of the natural sciences to understand, not to outwit, nature. I am often told that this or that is an "educated guess"—a truly nasty expression. Much would be gained if the guessers were educated instead. Some of the discussions on microbial heredity and chemical genetics that I have heard sounded like a bunch of midwives deliberating on the immaculate conception. And what can be done to stem the ever-growing avalanche of rubbish being published? I can think of only one way: publish all papers anonymously, without authors' names.

Y: By the way, the grapevine has told me that the code has been broken.

O: I hope someone keeps the pieces; one may need them again.

Y: How can you be facetious before such an achievement? Don't you see that we have entered a new era?

O: Thus, slowly, slowly, step by step, scream by scream, drum roll by drum roll, gold medal by gold medal, do you expect to reconstruct the fingerprints of God! But what good will it do you? You could not read them, you could not classify them. All the gimmicks in the world—to use the terminology with which you are familiar—will not help you.

Y: You talk as if we were still in the early Middle Ages.

O: Maybe the natural sciences will always be in the early Middle Ages. There goes a deep crack through our porcelain world; and even theoretical physics, perhaps the most highly developed science, feels, I am told, much malaise and intellectual discomfort. Could it be that molecular biology is the last refuge of the scientific optimist?

Y: Well, we have much to be optimistic about. This has been a marvelous period for the biological sciences, a true renaissance. We have learned more about life and heredity in the last five years than in the preceding fifty; and for this reason we can afford to disregard most of the older literature. Even you, who have difficulty in reconciling yourself to all our discoveries, will not be able to deny the tremendous upsurge.

O: There is so much to get reconciled to. In fact, that such very bad times as ours have given rise to so much good science, does this not speak against science?

Y: Not at all. You seem to have the romantically foolish idea that only a good man can be a goood scientist.

O: It is always dangerous to use the argument *ad hominem,* and you should not judge from yourself. It is getting late, though, and I had not quite finished with what I was saying before. Even if the correct code is found and the flow of so-called information takes place as postulated by the admirers of biological automation, very little of what occurs in a living cell is really clarified. That which determines the specific character of a cell, which is perpetuated in a hereditary fashion, consists of a very large number of different compounds, many of them situated specifically within the cell; and these substances, once we break the cell and isolate and separate its constituents, will be recognized as very many different species of molecules, such as proteins, lipids, polysaccharides, nucleic acids, etc. Most of those—and not only the first and last—have a highly specific composition and structure; but how they exist, interact and are held in definite places in the functioning cell is completely obscure. I am certainly no vitalist in the sense in which this is usually meant; but I cannot stomach people who claim that they have understood and explained *Hamlet* by telling me how often the word *and* appears in the first act. And I do object to the tremendous noise that is being made about trivial and often meaningless observations. In contrast to previous times, I believe, many of our reputedly great discoveries are entirely unearned. Also, the morass of alleged facts in which we are suffocating has brought it about that those who *may* speculate *cannot* do so any longer. Look at the enormous variety in the shapes of organisms, organs, even cellular components; where is the biochemistry of specific shape? Where is the biochemistry of cell differentiation? Is there a separate nucleotide code for your fingerprints, which are different from mine? Is it a pairing error in position seventy-nine which has produced the visions of Blake? Above all, it is against this shabby mechanization of our scientific imagination, which kills all ability to notice the unforeseen, that I protest—against this mat finish over a chaos of unrecognized ignorance, this butcher-like brutality with things that cry for gentle caution. Our young people are being brought up believing that "they never had it so good." They—and especially the best ones—are being condemned to a future of disillusionment and discouragement.

Y: That's what you say. I am not at all discouraged; quite the contrary. I only have to think of the unprecedented possibilities that are opening before us. When we know the Universal Code, we shall soon learn how to interfere with certain nucleotide sequences in DNA, how to change them specifically and thereby to produce desirable genetic changes. Artificial insemination with the stored sperm of dead geniuses has already been proposed by eminent authorities. Two little Einsteins in every middle class household. What a vista!

O: But can the centipede survive under a duodecimal system? The more you talk about breeding geniuses the less likely you are to get them.

Y: Again, one of your unscientifically mystical remarks. I only mentioned this proposal as a first modest feeler into the great future. Later on, we shall be able to look up the nucleotide sequence of every DNA; and each purine and pyrimidine will have a number; and we shall know of each what happens when we change it. And boy, will we change it!

O: And then you will get the real "human engineering." Once you can alter the chromosomes at will, you will be able to tailor the Average Consumer, the predictable user of a given soap, the reliable imbiber of a certain poison gas. You will have given humanity a present compared with which the Hiroshima bomb was a friendly Easter egg. You will indeed have touched the ecology of death. I shudder to think in whose image this new man will be made.

Y: Well, you may not be around to see it. Anyway, it was nice to have talked with you. I must still run up to the lab to turn off the Spinco.

O: Yes, the evening has come. I shall go home.

They leave, in opposite directions.

Ouroboros

. . . *Denn*
Wie du anfiengst, wirst du bleiben.[3]
Hölderlin, *Der Rhein* (lines 47, 48)

Le moindre mouvement importe à toute
la nature, la mer entière change pour
une pierre.[4]
Pascal, *Pensées* (Lafuma Nr.927)

The ashes of an Oak in the Chimney, are
no Epitaph of that Oak, to tell me how
high or how large that was; It tels me not
what flocks it sheltered while it stood,
nor what men it hurt when it fell.
John Donne, "Sermon Preached at
White-hall, March 8, 1622," *Selected
Prose,* E. Simpson, ed., (Oxford University Press, 1967), p. 210.

It is December, 1972. Two men—a Senile Chemist, S, and a Middle-aged Molecular Biologist, M—meet in the Metropolitan Museum.

S: Twelve years since we met last. Let's sit down on the sofa here. But what are all these packing cases doing here? The place is all cluttered up.

M: They are selling their old masters to make room for the new ones.

S: Just as in our sciences.

M: I fail to see the analogy.

S: Have you not noticed what an enormous change has taken place in our manner of quoting previous literature, in the way in which tradition is preserved in the sciences? I open the last issue of the *Journal of Molecular Biology* and pick a paper at random. It is even quite a good paper. There are twenty-nine references in it. Three are to papers published in the current year and all the others, with one exception, refer to papers published within the last five years. Compare this with any publication thirty, or even only twenty years ago. You will see what I mean when I say that the tradition has been broken.

M: This only shows that so much good stuff is published these days that there is neither the reason nor the room to refer to the older findings. Besides, these have lost all interest.

S: Precisely; we, too, are getting rid of our old masters. But there is a deeper significance to all this. If it is true, as one sometimes hears, that history is the memory of mankind— and this goes even more for the history of culture, of art or music or literature—then I must ask why this memory has ceased functioning in science.

M: This is quite simple. Science is the only intellectual activity in which there exists real progress. Artists or writers may change, they may be doing different things at different times; but only scientists advance.

S: Does this mean that all that went before must be forgotten?

M: Yes, and rightly so. We simply don't speak the same language any more. In addition, our young people despise history, except when writing grant applications where they have to describe the history of their subject.

S: This is, of course, no problem, for all their references are taken from one pot. Scientists nowadays make a modest living by taking in each other's bibliographies. Once a paper gets into the habit of not being quoted, it never will be. On the other hand, I know of one paper that has become the most quoted scientific publication; it gets lifted with every purloined bibliography and serves—like the silk fibers in a dollar bill—to guarantee historical authenticity.

M: You are overdoing this business of tradition and memory. It is a fact that science has moved more rapidly in the last twenty years than in all of its preceding history. Who cares about the neanderthalers of 1920?

S: I regret to say that you are probably quite correct. Yet, what good does it do to state that cancer research is spreading like a cancer or that virology is bursting the sciences it has invaded? I can only say that, whereas there may have been a time when science could not cope with the world, now the world can no longer cope with science. One of the two may have to go.

M: And it won't be science. But you have joined the silent majority: you have turned into an anti-intellectual. Who would have thought that? Besides, times are too serious and research money too hard to get for a scientist like you to go around and talk like this. Have you not heard what the official spokesmen of science have said? You don't want to be known as the first bird who fouled his own nest.

S: Far be it from me, though I like being a pioneer. I have, however, never been an admirer of the popular wisdom that directed me to go and foul other birds' nests.

M: Tell me, Senile, what makes you so bitter? Is it sour grapes, or what?

S: No, Middle-aged, I do not think so, though some grapes are indeed sour. I have often been asked this question, and my standard answer has been to refer the questioner to Shakespeare's sixty-sixth sonnet. It is just my form of protest against this bestial century. Call it, if you want, a "protective reaction strike."

M: Here you go using this disgusting slogan.

S: All slogans are disgusting. In this country we are born and we die with a slogan on our lips. The advertising industry—the true curse of our times—has polluted our brains with these little jingles; it has saturated them, and we carry their infernal aroma into our dreams. When I read the motto of the U.S. Strategic Air Force, "Peace is our profession," I felt like vomiting; and if I didn't, it was because I, too, am a child of this century. The world suffocates from false slogans that bleed true blood. The same friendly people that brought us the Final Solution now bring us the Protective Reaction Strike. You are right in not liking the slogan I used, though I was not in earnest. You might conclude, more charitably, that I want to be a witness, a voice for many others who may not have dared say it or were unable to find an audience.

M: Not that you have much of one. Really, I believe you are most unjust. In the last few years, science and especially biology have reached a depth that your generation, when you were young, could never have dreamed of.

S: Well, we had other dreams to dream. But since you speak about depth, I remember something I read recently in Pascal's *Pensées.* He reminds himself of what he ought to do: *Ecrire contre ceux qui approfondissent trop les sciences.*[5] He wants to write against those who go too deeply into the sciences, and he thinks of Descartes.

M: What nonsense! How can one go too deeply, too thoroughly into a thing? I always thought that you were peddling profundity. Is anything better for being done superficially?

S: This is, of course, not what Pascal meant. There is no telling beforehand which is more profound, the depth or the surface. Certain things must be explored in depth; in others not even the surface must be scratched. Nature must be investigated with respect, with reverence; it must be handled with, what in German is called, *Behutsamkeit*— a word inadequately translated into "caution," since it contains the element of *hüten,* to protect or to preserve.

M: Anyway, I have never cared for Pascal. If you want to stay in that century, give me Bacon.

S: Sure, there was a succulent man. "Knowledge is power." And power is what we choke on. It is the power of science that has strangled science. You see, this is what has happened. Science has been continuously splitting the pieces of the same old puzzle. The more pieces there are, the more difficult it is to put the puzzle together. Science is therefore a mechanism through which our worldview is being progressively fragmented.

M: Do you call the world a puzzle?

S: Well, I should rather call it a riddle. The more correct answers to a riddle there are, the greater the riddle. Only small riddles have a single solution. But what is so peculiar is that the mysteriousness of nature increases as one riddle after another is solved.

M: I don't buy that. I read in a recent bestseller that our knowledge about nature has increased to such an extent that there is no longer a necessity to believe in anything but chance.

S: Maybe. But what a picture! In the place of the *Fête de la Raison* of the French Revolution, we have here *Saint-Hasard* on a pedestal, freely pissing the thermodynamic consequences of programmed necessity on the bowed heads of the Worshipful Company of Molecular Biologists assembled all around. And not one of the coven who wakes up and says that it was all a bad dream.

M: And I who hoped that you had been reformed. I can only say what the "high-ranking military man" in the Pentagon said today in answer to complaints about the horrifying destruction of Hanoi and its population by American bombers: "So what's new?"

S: Indeed, is there ever anything new? Now that people are governed by their excrements, this excremental and at the same time infantile vision of the world has invaded all they are doing—art as well as science, poetry no less than biology. It is only fitting that the acrobat-comedians, as they hopped around the moon, announced their coming with the shout: "We is here!"

M: Well, even on Mount Olympus Apollo had many enemies, but they were the powers of darkness.

S: I wish I could sing as beautifully as the Queen of the Night. Speaking of "Apollo," for reasons unknown to me you can't get into a discussion of so called sophisticated methods of mass murder without touching upon Greek mythology. When a few bright physicists get together for a pleasant chat about how to kill the population of a country in a scientifically up-to-date way—lasers, sensors, and all that—this has to be called "Project Jason." O Gods of Colchis, I wish there were a "Project Medea" to wipe out the children of "Project Jason."

M: Here you won't get a peep out of me. I am only interested in biological engineering, in genetic surgery, the only surgery a Ph.D. is permitted to perform.

S: Perhaps we shall have time for that later. But what you said before about the tremendous increases in our knowledge about nature has interested me. I should say what you call knowledge about nature is habit-forming; the more one has, the more one needs. Those who search for knowledge about nature and those who seek truth about nature speak languages that are mutually unintelligible.

M: Obviously you believe that you belong to the second tribe.

S: It is certain that I do not speak for many. Whether they form a tribe or a tiny guerilla group hiding in the underbrush of more fashionable science, I do not know. Maybe I am all alone.

M: The more reason to shut up.

S: Soon, soon. But I should like to say one thing in all seriousness. After the Second World War, Adorno remarked that after Auschwitz poetry could no longer be written. Be that as it may, and perhaps that was the moment when real poetry should have begun; but it is clear that humanity could no longer sustain the necessary effort, and this is, I believe, true of all the arts. They have all been exsanguinated, as if it had been they who had been drained of the blood of the victims. I honor them for that: Silence may be the highest form of eloquence, failure the protective coloring of triumph. But what shall I think of our sciences? For ten years we have been sitting in what I would call the bargain basement of hell, before our eyes the trickle of blood out of the mouths and the eyes of mutilated children—truly an Auschwitz on the installment plan—and science growing heavier and better and always looking the other way, if not actively contributing to the misery and the shame. Our science, the wonder of the ages? Today the moon and tomorrow the universe? And not one vomit out of the learned lot.

M: This is not true. Many of us gave money to the campaign, and I wrote several letters to senators.

S: I know, many Germans painted their garden fences a very pretty light blue in protest against what the Nazis did; also the sale of books by ancient poets increased very much. This is not what I had in mind. What baffles me is that we grow better as we grow beastlier. Since there is no question about the beastliness, I begin to question the betterness. *Semen sanguis christianorum* [6]—but what Tertullian meant was that the blood of the Christian martyrs was the seed of their religion. If I said, *Sanguis semen scientiarum,*[7] this would also be correct, for science thrives on war and bloodshed; for a long time it has been living—and living very well—on the crumbs underneath the pentagonal table. The people would not support science if they thought of it as a matter of the mind, as an intellectual activity. It is the war potential of science—soon we shall celebrate Napalm Sunday—that has made it worthy of support.

M: Don't underestimate their fear of death either.

S: Yes, indeed.

> Our pleasance heir is all vane glory,
> This fals warld is bot transitory,
> The flesche is brukle, the Fend is sle:
> *Timor mortis conturbat me.*[8]

The fear of death, and not only on the part of aging senators, has always been a stronger cultural force than the love of beauty or of truth.

M: Therefore we are now having a national campaign against cancer. I have already applied for a big grant to study DNA-RNA hybridization in defective bacteriophage mutants.

S: If I were cancer I would take to my heels and flee. But seriously, this may well turn into one of the silliest boondoggles in history. If it were not tragic, it would be very comic. Even the signing of the act—the Great Fight Against Cancer—was turned into a technicolor spectacular: the GREATEST EVER! Imagine an invited assembly of society ladies, investment bankers—real and disguised as senators—and an immense gaggle of hungry assistant deans. And the whole thing presided over by prancing Heliogabalus or, should I say, Sporus in pancake makeup.

> This painted child of dirt, that stinks and stings.[9]

M: I have not heard Pope quoted since I was a sophomore. You have an encyclopedic knowledge of things that are of no use.

S: Thank you. And the bugles and the press releases, they trumpet of hundreds of millions of dollars. At the same time, the dollar crashes and all these streams of counterfeit gold soon thin to a trickle. In the end we shall have committees and committees of committees; huge collections of "position papers" will be published, circulated, and filed away in green cabinets bought for this purpose; the investment bankers will invest, the administrators will administer. And in the meantime, cancer sits in a tree and giggles. It is difficult to fight a war if you don't know your enemies, what uniforms they wear and how many there are.

M: Do you mean to imply that we don't know enough to fight an intelligent war against cancer?

S: Well, wars are never intelligent; but you are correct. The present idea seems to be that we shall select some huge forest and we shall declare that cancer is hidden in there somehow. We shall surround this forest with a huge force of hired beaters who will make a terrific racket to rouse and drive the hidden enemy. Whatever little animal comes running out will be given no quarter; it will be killed, and we shall declare that we have killed cancer. Then the chase will be called off. In the meantime, we shall never be sure that we have picked the right forest and that we have killed the right animal. In other words, we propose to attack cancer as if it were North Vietnam, carpet bombing and so on. The brutish and totemistic spirit of Dr. Fix-it is particularly unsuited for this sort of operation. "Crash programs" are more likely to crash the programmers than their objects.

M: Do you wish to say that we should sit and do nothing, and this with all the scientific unemployment?

S: Not at all. But more than anything else, we ought to beware of think tanks. For think tanks produce tank thoughts, and this is not the kind of thinking that will "conquer" cancer, if conquest is the right word. I have often wondered whether, behind the much advertised fight against cancer, there does not hide the real motive, namely, to abolish death (of course, for the right kind of people).

Are we ready for this? Well, I believe we are ready for anything. How about the abolition of death as a so-called national goal? But what a mess we shall be making! If we preserve the old, we shall have to kill the young. In fact, we have made a beginning in this direction.

M: I can't say that I understand you; but I seem to hear a senile death wish.

S: This may be so. But in my life I have seen too many ill-considered, harebrained schemes end in misery and total chaos to feel optimistic about our medical do-gooders who are ready anytime to apply the techniques for selling snake oil to the most profound, most unfathomable problems of life and death. Think of the transplantation debacle.

M: What a romantic you are! You seem to have some sort of mystical respect for man and for life.

S: You can even include dogs and cats and trees, and the rest of nature. We were talking of this before when I brought in the term *Behutsamkeit.*

M: If you had five hundred million dollars to spend, what would you do?

S: I won't tell you. But I would not spend them on contracts with a thousand chimpanzees to buy a thousand typewriters. Whatever statistics predict, I should not want to read their product.

M: But think of the input so many brilliant molecular biologists would have on the problem of cancer.

S: When I hear the word "input" I reach for my dictionary of clichés. But whatever "input" means, I am afraid cancer will be more useful to the problem of molecular biology than the other way around.

M: Well, what's wrong with this? Don't we all have to catch the sun where it shines and not wait till it comes to us?

S: I have always admired the celerity with which our scientists can turn around to catch the last ray of sunshine. But has not something gone wrong with science if its main purpose is to keep scientists employed? After all, the concept of truth did not come about in order to keep the seekers for truth in cigars. Suddenly, there are too many of us around; the world is becoming constipated with scientific facts, or what goes under that name. Nobody wants that many facts thrown at him at one time, always accompanied by an urgent request for an additional grant. The rule seems to be: no breakthrough without handout. So-called truth is apparently infinite; or, perhaps, this elastic commodity only masquerades as truth.

M: You sound like Mr. Youknowwho.

S: I should be sorry if I do; but who is the African statesman to whom you refer? Don't you see the absurdity of the situation? I often feel that it has been the ruin of science that it has almost become an American monopoly. This country has always had the tendency to blow up every balloon till it bursts. And now science has come to the bursting stage.

M: Can there ever be too much of a good thing?

S: Yes, there can. My favorite comparison is with music. Let us assume that there is a National Music Foundation in Washington and that this NMF makes large grants to many schools. These schools erect large buildings and fill them with pianos or electronic caterwaulers or whatever is needed to supply hundreds of graduate composers per year. Each of these students is now supposed to write a symphony every year of his fellowship support. What then? There is, of course, no audience for all this music; but since it exists, it has to be crammed down the ears of humanity. And after some time the musical moloch will demand a suitable supply of young people so as to have something to do. Anything said against this becomes an attack on the noblest inspirations of mankind; for who can be against music? There are many things in the world that cannot be institutionalized; but they are all about to become so—life and love, sex and art. Soon we shall have a Union of Dying People negotiating, presumably, for cheaper coffins.

M: Why not? Don't we live in a system of free enterprise? I should like to quote the greatest of all chairmen: "Let a hundred flowers bloom."

S: Well, I didn't know all this stench came from flowers. There is a great danger that America's entrepreneurs will also be its undertakers. Now the same kind of impresarios have invaded our sciences, and they get huge contracts for the production of facts. These facts can then be had as, what is called in the retail business, loss leaders. When I got into science, many years ago, I did it because I did not want to be in cloak-and-suit. And now I am in cloak-and-suit, right in the middle of the garment business.

M: But think of the enormous success of modern science.

S: Yes, we have all become hierophants of the bitch goddess. And what a cruel goddess this so-called success is. Just as the meowing machines of the music laboratories of which I spoke before, our laboratories, our journals, our societies, our institutes and universities have developed their own dynamism, their own *élan vital;* and out of disciples we have become slaves of a schizophrenic sibyl, and she has forgotten her Greek.

M: At least you have not forgotten your Pythian. How far we have strayed from talking about cancer research.

S: I am always willing to return to my malaise. If mission-oriented research were the solution, why not hire it out to one of our giant corporations, say, International Telephone and Telegraph? Maybe they could subvert the cancer cell. I have always had a great distrust of this sort of approach. After all, the best example of target-directed research is alchemy; and look at what mess they got into. The alchemists certainly consumed more gold than they made; but did one ever confess that he could not make gold? This *par force* chase of cancer under the leadership of a few molecular gurus looks comic to me. But who am I?

M: Surely you do not expect an answer. To tear down is easier than to construct. Do you have any ideas on how to go about it?

S: I am afraid what I have is not what you would call ideas. You are actually thinking of tricks, of stratagems, of a game plan. You are looking for ways around, for shortcuts. But for me disease, even cancer, is part of nature; and much as I dislike Francis Bacon in other respects, I have never forgotten his great words: *Naturae non imperatur nisi parendo.*[10] Only by obeying nature can you command her. I have often said that when the liver has cancer, the cancer has liver. Both are equally organic, and in many cases we may not be able to disentangle them. But before we can act—if act we should—we must understand them both; and I fear we do not know enough of either. I certainly do not object to research on this problem. In fact, a great deal of quiet, reticent, hard work will have to be done along with a great deal of silent thinking. What I object to is the song-and-dance approach and the innumerable symposia, held in the assorted beauty spots of the world—islands in the Aegean, Sicilian mountain tops, etc. How about a symposium in Harlem, on 125th Street? Would anyone come? But all this is childish; scientists, I hear, are human; and in a society as rotten as ours, not to be rotten is almost a sign of being dead. What I object to even more is that there is now great enthusiasm and massive support for what may be called a federal scheme for the spread of cancer.

M: This sounds even more bizarre than what you usually say. May I ask for an explanation?

S: I'll try to make it short. As you know, there is now much love for the concept that cancer in humans is due, or due in large part, to the presence in the organism of one of a series of viruses, the oncogenic viruses. The evidence is minimal, but the noise that is made is immense. The excitement is understandable, for here, many feel, there begins to appear, though in the vaguest of contours, a concept of the cause of cancer. There is, therefore, great interest in seeing more work done on these viruses. In Washington, they have begun to dismantle the entire scientific establishment of the country and turn over some of the remaining pieces to work on cancer. In fact, cancer research has itself become the best model of cancer, in the way it spreads and cannibalizes its surroundings. Millions of dollars are being contracted out to various institutions; factories are being remodeled to pose as cancer institutes. Every biologist who wants to survive must call himself a cancer specialist, and the experts in virology will preside over the distribution of the bounty. In many places these viruses will be grown in large quantities, in order to isolate their nucleic acids, their enzymes, and so on. Now, if these viruses really do as claimed, they must be among the most dangerous agents known. Yet they are being handled by people who are, at best, familiar with the completely innocuous bacteriophages and who have never been trained in the precautions required by highly infective material. The spray and the drippings from one such viral preparation ought to be enough to bring the blessings of cancer to the entire population. My only hope is that the basic hypotheses are wrong and that these viruses may only accompany, but not cause, the onset of cancer.

M: Don't think that we have not been worrying a lot about the very same thing. But what can one do about it? Where else would we get our support?

S: Yes, it is deplorable that our time goes through such rapid and unexpected convulsions that anti-technical or anti-scientific unemployment may take the place of what used to be called technical unemployment. The trouble is that, if quantity turns into quality, in science it turns very often into poor quality. We have produced too many angels that were only taught to dance on the heads of needles; and suddenly needles have become obsolete.

M: The more reason to rush wholeheartedly into the huge cancer boom. But you did not tell me how you would go about it.

S: To tell you the truth, I would rather go around it. Ours is the time of molecular biosemantics, and I should like to stay out of it. But I may give you some of the reasons of my skepticism. I am not at all sure that our way of looking at the problem is correct. My thinking—if you can call it thinking—goes as follows. When God created life . . .

M: God, GOD?

S: OK, OK, someone looking like Dr. Freud, wrapped in Darwin's plaid, sitting under a leafless tree; when He, She or It created life . . .

M: Nobody created life. You know that as well as I do. And where would the tree come from? Life is—how many authorities have told you so?—the child of chance and the father of necessity. We shall remain the slaves of life till . . .

S: Till?

M: No, I meant to say, forever. It is by accident that life arose out of the *Urschleim* . . .

S: It is getting late.

M: Out of the primordial soup, I say, there originated the first molecule endowed with self-replication . . .

S: You mean, it replicated itself with its own little hands?

M: Of course not. There came along a second macromolecule that helped the first to do its job, and from then on it was easier.

S: And a few years later it already played on the stock market. Inscrutable are the ways of chance. But, please, let me develop my argument, for whatever it is worth. I certainly do not want to step on your neo-positivist feet. Let us stay away from metabiophysics and move to neutral ground. When Monsieur Godot created life—or better, when he noticed that there was life—he must have said to himself: Whatever has a beginning must have an end.

M: Why?

S: In science you don't ask why, you ask how much. But in this case the answer is not too difficult. La Rochefoucauld said that man cannot look into his death as he cannot look into the sun.[11] He should perhaps have included birth as well. We get very dizzy when we look at beginnings or at ends, but we must do it. So Monsieur Godot, looking at the beginning, must also have contemplated the end. And while he rejoiced in all the teeming abundance of the innumerable forms of life, he programmed them all for death. He wrote death into their nucleus, so that we must all be rotting uphill toward the maximum of entropy.

M: I would not go that far. One could say that death has not yet been abolished.

S: I know. In science, the adverb "not yet" is the tribute that honesty pays to optimism. But short of an American national goal—"the impossible takes a little longer"—do we know how to abolish death, let alone the indescribable horrors that would ensue? In any event, I consider it as not impossible that all multicellular organisms carry this monogram of death which is cancer. So let me try this hyperbole: all men die of cancer at age 150, unless they have died of other causes, or even of cancer, before. And this is what usually happens.

M: Can you prove this grotesque hypothesis?

S: How could I? I lack sufficient experimental material, but you can't disprove it either. Actually, if I am correct, the National Campaign against Cancer is a campaign against death. I have spoken of this before.

M: But you know very well that many people die of cancer before they are 150, and even little children can get it.

S: Yes, I know, and it is actually with the children that I would start. If we really all carry this termination signal, then why is it triggered in some so much earlier? Therefore, I should first study the most aberrant cases, namely the young ones. I am not very hopeful that even this would lead to a cure. But before going on the hunt, we should at least be able to distinguish between the different animals much better than we are able now. Instead of shooting simultaneously in all directions—carpet bombing, as I called it before—I should like to define the target. But this is not good for technicolor spectaculars. Also I would not set up the whole thing as a five-year plan or whatnot. Even in the case of the moon I could have waited a good while longer without getting impatient. This is the most impatient country in history and it rushes from one mess to the next without waiting to catch its breath. Perhaps Rome in the time of the soldiers' emperors was similar; but both their wheels and their wheelerdealers turned much more slowly. Was there a campaign committee for the election of Caracalla? Maybe this was not necessary and his pre-imperial crimes recommended him directly for the succession. In any case, I never read that he was apprehended breaking into the *porta aquarum.*

M: I would not want to have your associations. I am told that this is the best administration since Harding.

S: This is quite possible. But I want to repeat: no worthwhile scientific discovery can be made with the hot breath of an entire nation and a malevolent government on the necks of the poor fellows who are paid to make it. To the extent that great scientific work is an activity of the mind— and there is a tenuous boundary where this is the case—it needs silence, it needs quiet, it must not be badgered. If Maecenas had every morning sent around to Vergil, even if only with a message of cheer, the *Aeneid* would never have been written. In a time like ours only the Devil can do significant work; he is not bothered easily.

M: Here I agree with you. There is not even money for foreign trips. Just when I had an invitation to a symposium at the Golgotha Hilton.

S: The Golgotha Hilton? That sounds apocalyptic.

M: Not at all. Just a NATO workshop on sinister forces.

S: I didn't know NATO went in for molecular eschatology. Incidentally, a few minutes ago I referred to the feverish and spasmodic pace at which everything is done in our time. I encountered a good example in something I read recently. The great philosopher Wittgenstein—perhaps I should call him the great mystic—who died only twenty-one years ago, spent the last two years of his life thinking about certainty, how he could know something to be certainly true. These notes were published after his death in a little book, *Über Gewissheit.* One of his remarks reads as follows:

Let us assume that an adult told a child he had been on the moon. The child tells it to me, and I say that this could only have been a joke; that So-and-so had not been on the moon, that nobody had been on the moon; that the moon was far, far away from us; and that nobody could climb up or fly there.—Yet, if the child insisted that, perhaps, there may be a way to get there which I did not know about, etc., what could I reply? . . . But a child usually will not cling to such a belief and will soon be convinced by what we tell him seriously. [12]

If this child was five years old in 1950 when these lines were written, he was just of the right age, when the first landing on the moon occurred, to die in Vietnam. Wittgenstein pursued his thoughts in many directions.

What we believe in depends upon what he have learned. We all believe that it is impossible to get to the moon; but there could exist people who believe that this is possible and happens sometimes. We say: these are ignorant of much that we know. Let them be as sure of this matter as they want—they are in error, and we know it. In comparing our system of knowledge with theirs, it is apparent that theirs is by far the poorer one. [13]

Well, for me not only their system of knowledge, but also their system of morals, have remained the poorer ones though it is they who have—but in whose sign?—conquered.

M: I am sure even you cannot deny that the multiple moon landings of the Apollo series represent the greatest triumph of science. In its entire history, science has had no greater one. Prometheus may have brought us the fire from the heavens; but we reciprocated. We have made the greatest dreams of humanity come true. We shall be known as the first generation that broke through the chains in which iron necessity has kept us bound hundreds of thousands of years. Think how far we have gotten since the first protein molecule recognized the first nucleic acid molecule.

S: I hope you use the word "recognize" in its biblical sense. I wonder in what language these two molecules conversed when they said "pleased to meet you." But when it comes to myths of creation, *Gilgamesh* reads better than the *Scientific American*, gorgeous as the prose of the latter usually is. Incidentally, you have forgotten to mention that as we climbed the peak of human history, we managed to land in the depth of a financial depression.

M: Who talks about money? Except, of course, in a grant application. This, by the way, is not the only triumph of science. Our century will be known as the Century of Biology.

S: I should have called it that of the Hundred-Years-War. Or perhaps the Century of Slaughter, as the Blackest of all Black Deaths, Hitler, fell like an axe from heaven on entire nations and races; and when his stiffening figure had to let go the breath of death, innumerable others all over the world applied, successfully, for his succession.

M: I stick to my name. We have learned all that is to be known about the mechanisms of heredity, at least in *E.coli.* We understand the chemical basis of biological information, we have broken the genetic code, we have isolated a gene, we have synthesized a gene. What have we not done? We know how proteins are made in the cell. I should say, we know all about everything.

S: Then I believe you ought to look for another profession.

M: Well, I may have been carried away. But even you can't deny that the concept of the messenger RNA alone will shine like a star in the history of science. It is a pity that it was not called Project Mercury; we could have gotten more money for it.

S: Yes, Mercury was not only the heavenly messenger, he was also the god of thieves.

M: Senile you really are impossible. It makes me sick to hear you talk like this, sort of anti-intellectual. And at the same time, I must confess I do not feel so good myself. To begin with, I read recently somewhere that the golden age of science is at an end, that we have discovered everything worth discovering, and that from now on we must reconcile ourselves to being second-raters. Does this mean that I won't get a laurel wreath?

S: It will have been a very short golden age, only a hundred years or so. Maybe it was only the gold-plated age of science. But I shudder to think what the real one will look like.

M: And in the second place, the people have turned against us. Science has become very unpopular; the silent majority hate us.

S: The silent majority hate everything.

M: Yes, but the young people have also turned against us, as if they didn't care to discover new laws of nature.

S: How many do you need? Congress must always make new laws because the people keep breaking the old ones. But the so-called laws of nature should last longer. I must, however, say that real science—not the mock science that you and I are practicing—is as inexhaustible as nature. What has not happened today can always happen tomorrow. Real science will always remain wide open. I am not even certain that we could recognize its practitioners; they are so very rare—a few in a century. If we ever meet again I shall try to explain to you what I mean. Now it is too late. You and I call nature that which we can measure; and it is difficult for us to escape the temptation to stretch particularities into generalizations. Our kind of science may well be in its last throes. The ruthless strip mining of nature; the imperialistic assault on the heritage of the world; the enslavement of all that should have made man freer; bestialization by knowledge; brutalization by fantasy; banalization of the deepest impulses of mankind; trivialization of all that must remain a mystery—can all this last much longer?

M: It will certainly outlast you. The greatest secret of nature is, perhaps, that there is no secret.

S: But this, too, is a secret.

M: Let's go. I still have to see the Spinco salesman.

S: We must leave together. There is only one way out.

They leave together.

Chimaera

. . . *flammisque armata Chimaera,*
Gorgones Harpyaeque et forma tricorporis
umbrae. [14]
Vergil, *Aeneid,* VI (288–89)

I am made to sow the thistle for wheat,
the nettle for a nourishing dainty.
I have planted a false oath in the earth; it
has brought forth a poison tree.
I have chosen the serpent for a coun-
cellor, & the dog
For a schoolmaster to my children.
I have blotted out from light & living the
dove & nightingale,
And I have caused the earth worm to beg
from door to door.

I have taught the thief a secret path into
the house of the just.
I have taught pale artifice to spread his
nets upon the morning.
My heavens are brass, my earth is iron,
my moon a clod of clay,
My sun a pestilence burning at noon & a
vapour of death in night.

Blake, Vala or The Four Zoas, Night the
Second, lines 387–96

In the rubble of M.I.T., in 1986. Smoke everywhere, occasional flames. Two figures are seen. The Old Molecular Biologist, O, buried to the waist in fuming debris, holds in one hand a battered copy of Current Contents; *in the course of the conversation he slowly extricates himself from the heap. On a small, slightly raised platform stands the black hooded figure of the Chemical Ghost, C; he is dressed like a Japanese puppet player.*

C: Taking a radioactive sitzbath? Or are you rehearsing a Beckett play? Anyway, welcome to the Stone Age!

O: Ai-ai-ai! Oink! Oink!

C: Please, stop humming this Stockhausen tune. From now on, we shall take the grunts of pain for granted and omit them. OK?

O: The voice sounds familiar, especially the accent; but I don't see anybody.

C: When we last met, there still was a Metropolitan Museum. Don't you remember?

O: You really are what I need now. What are you, a specter or something?

C: Yes, in the ultraviolet. But you will never see me again.

O: Good. I wish I would not hear you either. You should have my worries.

C: You would not gain by the exchange. Were we not told that we were entering the age of plenty, through science and technology? A synthetic chicken in every plastic pot? A nuclear toothbrush, an extermination oven on easy installments? Death abolished or, at any rate, deodorized?

O: Let's not rehearse recent history. There are not enough people left to remember. Crying over spilled nukes won't do any good.

C: Yes, the earth has become flat again. When I was still around I read a headline in *The New York Times* which said, "Men Report Seeing Edge of Universe." It was really one of my last good laughs, for I imagined a sign saying, "You are Now Leaving the Universe." And on the other side there was a sign saying, *Einstein ist kein Stein.* Now, the edge of the universe goes right through Cambridge. It appears, in fact, that humanity has seceded from the universe. It was no longer interested.

O: And just when my work was going so well. Tell me—I am really curious—up there, do they believe in DNA?

C: Well, I don't live—excuse me—I don't dwell exactly "up there"; but we hear a lot of grapevine. To answer your questions, they do believe in DNA, but they read it backwards.

O: You mean, reversed polarity?

C: No, plainly backwards.

O: A-N-D? What does this mean?

C: I am told that it's Swedish for "mind."

O: Why Swedish?

C: Since HE got the first Nobel Prize for Saintliness, Sweden has become very popular up there. But you probably know more about recent history than I do. I am a bit out of touch.

O: Do they really practice up there what I read in the gospel: "Kick them when they are down"?

C: In which gospel did you read that?

O: in the Gospel According to Saint Billy, of course.

C: Saint Billy? I never heard of this evangelist. That isn't the one who used to go around castrating rapists with his little pocket knife?

O: Well, it is the same. But later, after he got the Nobel Prize for Saintliness, he commissioned the Rand Corporation to design a gospel for him. It had a very big sale and had a lot of influence, even on people of other religions, such as the molecular biologists.

C: Although I have, of course, heard about the first award, I really do not know much about the whole thing. Tell me, this Nobel Prize for Saintliness, who gives it out?

O: Well, the Devil, of course, but not directly. Officially, it is some sort of Ecumenical Council of Malmö which is supposed to vote on it each year. But in reality, it was the Devil who had this idea, and he went to ITT, and they fixed it for him.

C: ITT? Is that something like the Id of the psychoanalysts?

O: Yes and no, but it is certainly even more lucrative. The amount of good they have done—mostly to themselves—cannot be measured.

C: Then why did they not get this funny Nobel Prize?

O: So far it has not gone to corporations, only to individuals. But a few presidents of conglomerates may be in line. The Council loves to honor men who live dangerously, always on the brink of somebody else's disaster.

C: Truly, in the world which has now terminated, it must have been difficult to decide where stock speculation ended and sainthood began. The way from the ridiculous to the criminal went through the sublime, and often the three were mixed together. Since nobody had anything to compare himself to, the gray and bleak appearance of life was like a reflection in a blind mirror. Everybody grappled and did not know with what; nobody wept, nobody remembered; memory was a leaf buried in cement. If you are still alive, I weep with you.

O: Your tears must be as insubstantial as your body.

C: Since all sense of value had become obliterated, since even the recollection of what human behavior could signify had disappeared, and even the memory of this memory, rank and weight were assigned on the grounds of chance. Instant genius, instant sainthood became available to the highest bidder. The old and safe precept—only a dead saint is a good saint—was no longer followed. Scoundrelism became the last refuge of the patriot. A depraved type of chauvinism, the lowest form of *lumpen* patriotism, had taken over the land. "Look at us!" the American billionaires cried to their fellow citizens: "Look at us! You are the richest people in the world." And they looked and looked, affixed to their television screens, and were proud.

O: May I interrupt the charming word painting and complain about my intolerable situation? My limbs are all numb.

C: This is only the beginning. But I think we agreed to take your suffering for granted. Animal spirits cannot be admitted here where we deal with the highest.

O: Why, ghost, this is hell!

C: You are not quoting Marlowe, are you? Anyway, you don't know at all what hell is. Wait, wait.

O: Do you?

C: I have a vague notion, but it is impossible to convey it to an aspirant. I must speak in allegories. Hell is a university very much like Columbia—or maybe I exaggerate—let us say, very much like Harvard.

O: Have I not read somewhere something similar?

C: Yes, when you were a sophomore.

O: Do you think there will ever be science again?

C: Why, the entire world has become a proving ground for the most interesting studies on radioactivity, an immense laboratory for radiation work on humans. Think how many volumes were written on Hiroshima alone, how many commissions were sent to investigate the victims of the greatest scientific discovery of all times; that is, until yesterday came along. Now, I am not so sure, for will there be a tomorrow? In any event, whatever happens, it will not be the same science that you and, more reluctantly, I have been practicing.

O: For God's sake, what really happened?

C: Not much has happened lately for God's sake. In fact, numerous divines have assured me that He is dead. They have, however, never told me that the same is true of the Devil. Was there a bestseller, *The Devil Is Dead?* He is the enemy of nature, the Great Empty One. The old saying can be turned around: *Vacuus abhorret naturam.* He has a very pragmatic mind, although he cannot afford to be a statistician. He is truly target-directed; every sin is credited from the day of deposit. He is the patron—patron saint would be too much—of the efficiency experts. Nothing has ever been as effective as the dissembly line over which he presides.

O: I must ask you again. Will there ever be science?

C: Well, "ever" is a long word. I could ask in return: was there ever science? I know there were lots of scientists. Too many, in fact, as we were assured by some of our leading statesmen who had probably flunked freshman chemistry. To answer all the questions that I can half-hear between your cries of agony, I should have to take a long breath. All true dialogues are monologues. So, this one will have to become one too for some time.

He pulls out several sheets of paper and starts reading.

Monologue of the Chemical Ghost on the End of Art, the End of Science, the End of Everything

I

Many may say that the misery began with the French Revolution. I do not believe so, although, Joseph de Maistre, for instance, was of a different opinion, and I do not take his opinion lightly. To begin with, the French Revolution was successful, at any rate in part, and it was necessary. The world is not governed by the ridiculous idea of progress —after all, it must have been much nicer during the *aurea aetas,* not to speak of paradise—but it is governed by change. And if change is repressed or impeded for several centuries, an explosion becomes necessary, and it is better if it makes a very big hole. This is what happened then; and Goethe, though not a particularly perspicacious political thinker and very much out of sympathy with the revolution, saw it clearly when witnessing the cannonade of Valmy in 1792; he announced forthwith the beginning of a new epoch in history. It was, however, at that time that regime by committee came about; that vapid oratorical gesticulation—so dear to the less gifted half-brother of the French Revolution—took over; that all thoughts began to be talked into mush which often was not untinged by blood. It was also about that time that the viscous river of twaddle began to flow: the dailies, weeklies, monthlies, and, later and even more nefariously, broadcasting and television. The onset of the gigantic opinion industry, and the associated brain laundries of the advertising industry, are surely the blackest plague that has ever been inflicted on mankind; they have paralyzed human conscience and consciousness; they have "tenderized" the brain and the heart.

In other words, the young and rising bourgeoisie began to perceive the dawn of a rich and enriching day; but it was by no means sure that it would live to enjoy it. The essentials of this period are, perhaps, best revived for us in such novels as Stendhal's *Le Rouge et le Noir*, Flaubert's *L'Education Sentimentale* or Goethe's *Die Wahlverwandtschaften*.

II

It is, however, the year 1848 that in many respects appears to me to be the date when our times, the modern era, really started. For it was then that everything began to go wrong. Had the 1848 revolutions succeeded in France, Italy, Austria, Germany, etc., or at least in a few of those countries, instead of suffering abysmal failure everywhere, we should be living in a very different world. Revolutions seem to require a second edition, abbreviated and brought up to date, just as a spaceship, to be kept in orbit, often requires the detonation of small supplementary rockets. This could have been the function of the abortive revolutions of 1848. Pseudo-upheavals, such as those that took place in Germany, Austria, etc. at the end of the first world war, hardly qualify for attention; they appear to have occurred under the motto: "In case of rain the revolution will take place in the hall."

Of course, each moment in history, each historical epoch, represents, in many respects, the decadence of the preceding one; and retrospective integration must lead to a view that, though correct for the whole, is false for any particular. The common view of the *Biedermeier* period as one of satisfied quietism only testifies to the efficacy of censorship and police supervision.

In any event, the temporary and largely ostensible suspension of stress and tension vanished in 1848. Europe lost its last chance to do away with the deadening regime of the moneyed bourgeoisie, with the self-propelling, giant spider's net of mercantile and industrial entrepreneurs. The tone of the times changed abruptly, and with it came the first massive alienation of the spiritual forces from the dominant society. The extreme feeling of homelessness has been growing since, but I believe it was then that it began. Goethe or the Humboldts, David and Ingres, were at home, but Victor Hugo and Daumier, Flaubert, Baudelaire, and Rimbaud were not. In Germany and Austria, the separation began, if anything, earlier: with Kleist and Hölderlin, Büchner and Nestroy.

III

If I were asked which publications were typical for this period, I should mention two that I consider quintessential. One is very widely known, and most college students have read it. This is the *Communist Manifesto* by Marx and Engels. The other one probably has been read by very few and has had, in contrast to the first, very little effect; but I think it is more important, not on historical, but on philosophical grounds. It is a little brochure, not much more than one hundred pages, which Kierkegaard published in 1846 under the title *En literair Anmeldelse*. It represents itself, as the title indicates, as a book review, and the first part is, indeed, a painstaking discussion of what had attracted Kierkegaard's interest in a recently published story. The second part is, however, something entirely different; it consists of an incredibly acute dissection of the trends and tendencies of what then was "the present age." This portion of the book was translated into German by Theodor Haecker under the title *Kritik der Gegenwart* (Innsbruck, 1922) and into English by Alexander Dru under the title *The Present Age* (New York, 1962).

The book is not easy to read; the dense writing is crabbed in places—perhaps not more so than would be expected of a philosopher who had listened to Schelling's last lectures in Berlin—but one is often rewarded by passages that take one's breath away. The first sentence of the section sets the tone:

> Our time is essentially the time of intelligence, of reflection and dispassion, exploding superficially into enthusiasm, reposing shrewdly in indolence.

It is a time that has lost all passion, all intensity. Everything is prevented from happening, though it always looks as if much went on. "That a man stands and falls with his deed has become obsolescent." "The entire age has become a committee." Whereas before it was up to the individual to act, now we have only advertisements and shallow reports of *faits divers.* The time is full of tensions, but the elasticity is gone. And so Kierkegaard concludes that "a revolution would be most inconceivable in our time." If action on the part of the individual—the only kind that he recognizes—has become impossible, a catastrophic leveling process has produced the notion of "the public."

> For leveling really to occur, there must first be produced a phantom, the spirit of leveling, an enormous abstraction, an all-embracing something which is nothing, a mirage—this phantom is called *the public.*

> Produce twenty-five signatures under the most stupid thing, and you have an opinion; whereas the best-founded opinion of an eminent head will be considered a paradox.

IV

The processes that initiated the decline of Western civilization; the anonymatization, the statistification of all reactions of the human heart and mind; the replacement of the individual by a social security number; the substitution of public for individual opinion (a single neck for Caligula to wring), the fragmentation of society into pressure groups and lobbies; the nebulous power of the press and the "media" over an equally nebulous public; the erosion of the will, the dignity, and the responsibility of the individual; the debunking of everything great, thus preventively defusing all enthusiasm—all this, and much more, Kierkegaard foresaw clearly.

It is not an accident that such terms as "outsider" or "misfit" in their present connotations came into use at about that time and, I believe, first in America.

It is the privilege of the great religious thinker to predict the impending Martyrdom of the Ten Thousand, the coming slaughter of the millions of innocents, after reading some newspaper gossip about what Frøken Gusta said last night in a theater box to Frue Waller. There have been others who later spoke to the same theme with equal intensity, and they were equally unheard: Léon Bloy, Karl Kraus, Péguy, Bernanos. They all knew that the world can die from abstractions, from slogans that suddenly start to bleed from their mouths.

Abstraction applied to the individual creates apathy; he becomes as gray as he is painted to be. Despite the lassitude and lethargy which Kierkegaard recognized as the tribute that mass man pays to mass society, intellectual activity—always the prerogative of the single brain—and artistic production continued gloriously. France, and somewhat later central and northern Europe, lived through one of the greatest periods in the history of the arts; there was much great writing and great poetry. But the greatest of these artists and writers were forced to claim a form of extra-territoriality that would have been unthinkable before. They were no longer at home in their country and many not even in their language.

V

Science—or at any rate the kind of science that those of us who are now old encountered in their youth—began at this time of incipient estrangement, and this may not be without significance. This was the time of the professional; and the ever-growing trend toward specialization led to the creation of many university chairs for the various sciences and later to the formation of the first institutes devoted exclusively to scientific research.

In fact, some of the key words received their characteristic connotations around that time. Here are the approximate dates from the *Oxford English Dictionary: expert*, 1858; *professional*, 1848; *specialist*, 1862. *Public opinion*, in its present sense, was used earlier.

It is usually stated, and with some justification, that modern science originated in the time of the late Renaissance when it could be defined as the armed branch of philosophy. But, though the impulses that drove them to the study and later the exploitation of nature may always have been the same, up to the middle of the nineteenth century the men that devoted their lives to science were not the sort of scientists with whom we now are familiar. Many, in fact, did not really devote their entire lives to science, carefully maintaining their amateur status. It is difficult to decide whether, for instance, Descartes should be considered a philosophical genius, a good geometrician, or an indifferent anatomist. Was Newton a physicist or a biblical exegete? Was Kepler an astrologer, a theologian, a calendar-maker or an astronomer? Was Paracelsus a genius-quack or one of the founders of pharmacotherapy? Was Pascal a religious thinker, a mathematician, the inventor of the calculating machine, or the organizer of the first bus service? Was Kant a cosmogonist or a philosopher? They were all great men —great in what they did and in what they did not do—and they avoided hanging silly labels on themselves.

But, in a somewhat later day, Hegel and Schopenhauer were philosophers, Wöhler and Liebig organic chemists, Gauss a mathematician. And when it comes to our time, a man may well be an expert on the flagella of one kind of bacteriophage. Small lice, I suppose, are always infested with even smaller lice; but one should have thought that there must be a limit somewhere. Actually, there is not, though intellectual rentability may decrease with the decimals.

There exist, of course, many exceptions even in our time; Nietzsche and Houseman, Valéry, Bertrand Russell or Sartre could appear in several very different professional dictionaries. But what is this when compared with the life and work of a Leibniz or a Wilhelm von Humboldt?

When the cobbler became a shoe specialist, comfortable shoes could no longer be found. As man was being divested of his individuality—a reversal of the mysterious process of individuation which has agitated many philosophical minds—he became increasingly eligible for being given a number and a label. His soul was declared nonreturnable, not even fit for being recycled. This was the way to Auschwitz, Belsen, Buchenwald and the rest of the infernal ABC. What was left of the victims were their gold teeth, and those could be recycled.

VI

What had happened? The simplest answer—but one entirely unacceptable to the scientific mind—would be that sometime around the end of the fifteenth century the Devil moved his office from, say, China to western Europe. I am fully aware that I lack any acceptable proof; besides, there are no suitable controls. History is the typical "one-shot experiment," since it can never be repeated under standard conditions. It is, therefore, better to forget about explanations that appeal to the childish mind and to point out that in most sciences the question "Why?" is forbidden and the answer is actually to the question "How?" Science is much better at explaining than at understanding, but it likes to mistake one for the other. Even Kierkegaard offered no remedy for the sickness that he diagnosed so perceptively; salvation—one of the proscribed words of our time—could come only through the unconditional surrender of the individual to divine majesty. But where are these single ones? The English language even lacks a word that corresponds closely to the Danish *hiin Enkelte* or the German *der Einzelne*.

Kierkegaard, whose dialectics were of an entirely different kind, disliked Hegel. He could not reconcile himself to the glib process in which the interplay of thesis and antithesis leads to a synthesis that often is no more than the feeble acceptance of the lowest common denominator as consensus. He believed in the jump from the fire into the water; and it would not have occurred to him that the mixing of the two elements may be more practical. He was not a practical man; he was not a democrat; he might have felt that with the introduction of universal suffrage everybody lost his vote. It could be said of him, as of every inspired man, that it was the wilderness that gave rise to the crying voice. And he was the first to diagnose the existence of a desert right in the middle of little Copenhagen. Since his time, the sands have been growing at a frightening speed.

VII

The dissociation between sensibility and reason set in around the turn of this century. The time of computerized mass slaughter approached, preceded by the time of mass entertainment, mass transport, and the many other things of which it could be said that the application of the term "mass" serves to drown out, denature, and finally destroy the *vox humana*. Certain activities—art and even science—still resisted the prefix. The denaturation of language had begun, but not yet the denaturation of nature.

Painting, music, and literature are more sensitive to irreversible decline than is the individual. At the risk of some exaggeration, one could say that the last painter who *saw* a tree was Cézanne. A corresponding statement in music could be made of Debussy; just as Theodor Fontane or Knut Hamsun were, perhaps, the last novelists to see man in a human way. But the center did not hold; harmony and landscape, the human face and heart, the forms of people and of things, the coherence of thought in language were all distorted and torn apart. The dehumanization of man preceded the denaturation of nature. Pastiche and persiflage—bleeding tongue in swollen cheek—had taken over. Art and writing had to become hermetic to ward off a reality that was intolerably ugly. With Proust and Joyce, with Mahler and Schönberg, with Matisse, Picasso, and Braque, a terminal era seemed to have begun. Poetry, the most vulnerable of occupations, succumbed to a progressive desiccation.

The sciences, too, were distorted, but in a different way: they started to swell. Their philosophical basis had never been very strong. Starting as modest probing operations to unravel the works of God in the world, to follow his traces in nature, they were driven gradually to ever more gigantic generalizations. Since the pieces of the giant puzzle never seemed to fit together perfectly, subsets of smaller, more homogeneous puzzles had to be constructed, in each of which the fit was better. In the process, the various scientific disciplines had lost their common language. When they wanted to speak to each other, they had to resort to a form of Esperanto called mathematics; and finally, they had to limit themselves to expressing only what could be said in that language. The mathematization of the sciences, completed in this century, rendered them more exact, but often placed several layers between them and reality. The general loss of the sense of reality in our time has been accelerated powerfully by the growth of the sciences.

Other influences had also begun to operate. They emphasized the ambiguous position that science occupied from its very beginning. Whereas the other intellectual activities of mankind—I could list the entire *studium generale*—were supposed to contribute to making a better man or a happier man, science was presented as being able to make a richer man. Science could be used, for better or for worse; and it was usually the latter. A scientist who nowadays asserts his harmlessness ought to be fired for incompetence. The enormous growth of industry in the second half of the nineteenth century saw uses for science, or at any rate for certain sciences. There was a need for engineers and for chemists, and these occupations first started to swell and later took the other sciences along. The scientific professions began to develop a momentum of their own, thereby creating a vested interest in always having more science, bigger science, better endowed science. This is, incidentally, quite in contrast, for instance, to orchestra musicians whose influence on the number of orchestra pieces being written is minimal.

VIII

Despite this forced growth, no one who entered science after 1945 or 1950 can understand how small the scientific establishment really was in comparison to our times. The second world war and, even more, the gruesome "cold war" elevated it to the precarious and presumably untenable position of the seventies. It was probably the entrance of the United States on the world scene that created the trap of which they are now—without any chance of success—trying to liberate themselves by inviting the mice to go away. Being imbued from their youth with the notion that bigger is better—a principle that already led the dinosaur to disaster—they tried to apply it to matters of the mind that cannot tolerate it. If science is the search for truth about nature, there is no possible plan that could tell me how many scientific facts have to be discovered per year. Are six laws of thermodynamics better than three?

The pullulation of so-called scientific facts has been particularly noticeable in biology. I have an old maxim: "scientific truth is what has not yet been disproved." But disproving takes so much longer than proving, and in the meantime the brain is swamped with much more information, be it provisional, evanescent or trivial, than it can incorporate. This has led to a truly intolerable situation: the practitioner of a science must know much more than he can know. Ignorance is no handicap in the arts—Renoir did not have to have seen all the nudes that were painted before him—but in the sciences, always fighting at an ever-shifting frontier, this spells the end. One should have thought that what is called "negative feedback control" would operate, so that the people would have to spend so much time reading the papers of others that they would have no time to write their own. But this hope was extinguished many years ago when I discovered that scientists operate in two compartments: those who write do not read, those who read do not write. As it happens, then, the cat was not so much killed by curiosity as by the mass of information that its curiosity elicited. "Less is more," in science as in architecture.

Thinking about the horrendous misdeeds of our science and our technology—the atomic bomb, the landing on the moon—and dreaming, not in joyful anticipation, of the super-supersonic airplane soon to come, it was with a feeling of deep melancholy that I came upon the following passage in a play produced in London in 1605:

> These hastie advancements are not naturall; Nature hath given us legges, to goe to our objects; not wings to flie to them.
>
> Chapman, Jonson, Marston, *East-ward Hoe*, II, 1

IX

Our time is essentially the time of torpor, of action and thought by delegation, exploding vicariously into violence, relapsing emptily into boredom and despair. (Compare the quotation from Kierkegaard in part III of this section.)

More could be said, just as Kierkegaard could no doubt have said more in 1846. He saw a savior for the single man, I do not; I am ninety-two years more tired than he could have been. The revolution that could liberate man, at any rate Western man, from his predicament—if revolution is the right word—cannot even be foreseen. The potions to cure the sickness that have been prescribed—usually mixtures taken from the medicine cabinets of the two great doctors of our times, Marx and Freud, both much better at diagnosis than at therapy—give me little hope of success, even when an ounce of Zen has been added.

It is easier to dwell on the symptoms, and I have done some of this before. The conversion of humanity into a machine of continuous consumption and defecation has made the world dirtier, not happier. The most frightening symptom that I have encountered is that man is beginning to lose his relationship to language. I am thinking of a process similar, and possibly parallel, to that of disindividuation that I have already mentioned. This has nothing to do with the knowledge of spelling, the gift of tongues, etc.; it is an almost epidemic and progressive aphasia which, I believe, started in America and is now spreading.

A few more remarks could be added. Life and all its functions have become a spectator sport; many millions could now watch the crucifixion on their television screens. They would be unimpressed, though a few might write letters to their congressmen. Humor, the only detour around the world, has vanished; it has become so black as to be invisible. Our time operates under what I have called the Devil's Maxim: what can be done, must be done. And I shudder to think of all that can be done.

The arts, the only true fever thermometer of a period, indicate the approaching end. Science has become an eye without a head, a desperate attempt to fill holes with gaps. It came up to a lock, so it looked for the key; but it was a lock without a keyhole. The priests of truth are soiled with blood;their discoveries have become inventions, their pledges far from eternal. In a science in which one can say "this is no longer true," nothing is true.

I shall end with the sound of a sad trumpet:

Filiae Hierusalem, nolite flere super me: sed vos ipsas flete, et super filios vestros. Quoniam ecce venient dies, in quibus dicent: Beatae steriles, et ventres qui non genuerunt, et ubera quae non lactaverunt. St. Luke, 23, 28, 29

C: Why have you been so quiet all this time? I thought you would interrupt me. Have you been asleep or simply full of silent admiration? Just to wake you up, I believe there may be a Spinco left in New Zealand.

He is joined by a second black-hooded figure.

C: Well, then there is no way out.

Complete darkness

Epilogue in the Labyrinth

The speakers are Minotaur and Ariadne.

Minotaur: Welcome, sister. It must be a thousand years since you came to see me. How is the world outside?

Ariadne: If you had consulted a good handbook of Greek mythology you would know that you should not call me sister.

Minotaur: Is not Pasiphaë—she who shines for all—your mother and mine?

Ariadne: Here in Crete we don't follow the *Code Napoléon*, and it is the father who counts. Mine is King Minos, I want you to remember, and yours just a white bull.

Minotaur: "Just" is an understatement. My father, the White Bull, is usually capitalized. He is every bit as mythological as the rest of our family. But never mind, I shall not even call you "half-sister," as I have every right to do; I shall call you Ariadne. So tell me, Ariadne, what are the voices I hear?

Ariadne: This must be the latest shipment of young men and women that you have been extorting from Athens, from time immemorial, to devour them, suck their blood, and whatnot. Some of them always get lost in the labyrinth. But I am sure you know how to find them.

Minotaur: Ah, a new bunch of graduate students, unspoiled, enthusiastic, bringing new forces to exploring the old labyrinth. How I love to work with these young minds. There is so much to do, and the labyrinth grows all the time. No sooner have we explored one spiral than we find that it has branched out into a hundred new ones. Truly, I inhabit the never-ending, the ever-expanding labyrinth. I am the lord of the fruitful complications.

Ariadne: You are nothing of the kind. You are a blood-thirsty monster. That's what you are supposed to be, it's in all the books. Your poor victims, do you call them graduate students? A nice kind of study, to be eaten alive by a hypo-critical moloch.

Minotaur: Please, don't mix the mythologies.

Ariadne: How I wish Theseus would come and slay you.

Minotaur: The old fool must be here very soon. It is almost a thousand years since he last killed me. And he never loses his youthful vigor, the idiot, and goes through all the required motions as if he didn't know that shadows cannot slay each other. This tenebrous Crete of ours is the kingdom of dreams and reflections. What never lived, lives forever. The mirror that was broken before it reflected the image must reflect it to the end of the times. We shadows burn in a sun that never sets. There is an indescribable magic in what never happened. Ariadne, Ariadne, don't you remember your future?

Ariadne: Alas, I do.

Minotaur: Don't worry, there are, as usual, several versions. I, at any rate, remember vividly, if this is the *mot juste,* what will happen to me. I cannot wait for Theseus to come and slay me, so that I can at last get on with my work.

Ariadne: You keep on talking about your work, as if you did any more than to crunch children, you horrid bull-man.

Minotaur: Please note that, if this were true, it would be the man in me, not the bull, who would be doing this. My fa-ther was a herbivore. But you really have no idea of what I am doing.

Ariadne: Then what is this work that you pretend to do?

Minotaur: I explore the labyrinth, I search for the truth about this miracle of beauty in order, of predictable har-mony. This universe of mine, in which I have been placed—who knows why?—I shall never have certainty about it; but I feel I am getting nearer to being able to describe it. I may even publish a book. The labyrinth is different in daytime than it is at night. It is bigger than big, it is smaller than small. Nobody can encompass it all, for it keeps on growing, and not only on its edges. It changes as does the mind of minotaurity. I shall call my book *Minotaur Evolving.*

Ariadne: To me it doesn't look like much. Just a jumble, a hodgepodge of curlicues. And it stinks of rotting flesh and blood. To reach you I had to stumble through a gigantic maze of blind alleys, pitch-black and reeking, and then suddenly the blinding radiance surrounding you.

Minotaur: I can see that you lack the scientific mind. I hope you at least have not forgotten to unwind your skein of DNA, so that you can find your way back to the overworld. For it is only this thread, Ariadne, that will permit you to return to irreality.

Ariadne: You call this world of mine, to which I shall be returning, unreal? This world of rising and setting suns, of wind in olive trees, of children and lovers, of music and honey, of sorrow and joy—you call it unreal? Then what is the reality of the labyrinth? What is your reality?

Minotaur: Reality is what I can measure and what I can weigh. What are the dimensions of your wind? And even if I knew the weight of your olive tree, what good would it do me? In my branch of eternity one asks only questions that can be answered or, even better, one determines the answers first and then one poses the carefully selected questions. You can't imagine how much thinking has gone into this. Reality is what I can describe and what I can repeat. You could object that an ordinary son of Crete cannot describe, and certainly cannot repeat, his birth and his death; and you could ask whether this means that these are unreal. I would say yes; the beginning and the end have always seemed to me to carry an aroma of irreality. They lack the trivial, the automatic, the banal character of what is repeatable.

Ariadne: But do you only measure and weigh?

Minotaur: No, I also create. I make square what is round; I make round what is square. I order the world into right-handed and left-handed screws. Anything goes, with moderation, as long as I can express it in an equation.

Ariadne: Who taught you all this mumbo jumbo?

Minotaur: A truly unclassical question. Why, of course, it was Daedalus; he laid the groundwork of this labyrinth of mine, though it has since grown so much that he would not recognize it. You should have seen him. Here was a really great engineer. His only sacrifices were to science and progress. I often heard him say that he only believed in what worked. But then the poor man got into family trouble. You know, the generation gap.

Ariadne: You must be so busy devising equations that you don't seem to notice in what a mess you are living. Not a breath of air, the horrible stench, and blood spattered all over the walls.

Minotaur: Just wait. I shall sweeten the air with synthetics; I shall create a completely novel atmosphere. I shall cover the walls with plastics that are washed easily. I am so creative that I simply have no time to get around to such minor matters. There are so many more important things. I am making a catalogue of the pitch of all the spirals in the labyrinth. New ones are growing all the time, and each is different. But there must be a law underlying all this, and I shall arrive at a generalization that will apply to all future labyrinths. I am on the verge of proving the selective advantage of left-handed spirals, and I believe there is the principle of the survival of the fittest side corridors.

Ariadne: In the meantime you don't seem to mind that your roof is coming down all over your filthy warren.

Minotaur: I know, I know. But there is help around the corner. The Academy has just today sent me the list of their committees. Let me read you the name of one of those.

AD HOC ADVISORY PANEL FOR AN EXPLORATORY PROGRAM TO ESTABLISH THE FEASIBILITY OF INITIATING A MAJOR EFFORT TO DEVELOP NEW TECHNOLOGY SOLUTIONS TO ROOFING PROBLEMS IN DEVELOPING COUNTRIES [15]

Isn't this truly a crescendo, building up from the first cautious and probing steps, so befitting a scientist, to the major glory of lasting achievement? Not that anything is going to come of it, except so-called position papers, and the countries will have to continue developing unroofed. But is it not beautiful to sit on the seashore watching the huge breakers rolling in, even if they do no useful work? Incidentally, if you want to refer to this committee, I suggest, for reasons of euphony and brevity, to call it AHAPEP.

Ariadne: The people of Knossos know how to build roofs. And no committee has ever built a roof. I am afraid, beast, your ideas of reality and mine are totally different. You live in a labyrinthine world of your own making, and we others, once we enter it, shall never find the way back.

Minotaur: Well, the original construction is not mine, and it really was not very much when I first got here. Only later did it get so beautiful, when I began to build labyrinthories. But don't you see how consistent all concepts about the labyrinth are? In fact, the labyrinth has begun to adapt itself to my ideas about it. It grows where I say. It will spread over the island, over the world, over the universe.

Ariadne: Oh, how I wish Theseus would come and slay you!

Minotaur: You know as well as I do that this is useless, and I shall return to an even more splendid labyrinth. But I must say, these continuous interruptions, every thousand years or so, are a nuisance. I shall have to invent an anti-Theseus, and then I shall be free forever.

Ariadne: Why not instead an anti-Minotaur?

Notes

CHAPTER TWO
A Quick Climb Up Mount Olympus

1. J. D. Watson, *The Double Helix*
2. *Ibid.*, p. 26.
3. *Ibid.*, p. 66.
4. *Ibid.*, p. 136.
5. *Ibid.*, p. 4
6. *Ibid.*, p. 184.
7. *Ibid.*, p. 199.
8. *Ibid.*, p. 181.

CHAPTER THREE
Preface to a Grammar of Biology

1. Thomas Love Peacock, *Gryll Grange*, chapter 19.
2. Jean Paul, "Dämmerungen für Deutschland," in *Sämtliche Werke* (Berlin: Reimer, 1862), vol. 25, p. 91. A similar passage may already be found in Montesquieu, in the 105th letter of his *Lettres persanes*.
3. E. Diehl, *Anthologia lyrica Graeca* (Leipzig: Teubner, 1949–52), Nr. 103.
4. Taken from the German translation: Søren Kierkegaard, *Die Tagebücher* (Innsbruck: Brenner-Verlag, 1923), vol. 2, p. 33.
5. Friedrich Miescher, *Die histochemischen und physiologischen Arbeiter*, 2 vols. (Leipzig: F. C. W. Vogel, 1897). The letters collected in the first volume and also the introduction by Wilhelm His are particularly worth reading.

6. R. Taton (ed.), *Histoire Générale des Sciences* (Paris: Presses Universitaires de France, 1961), vol. 3, pt. 1.

7. E. Chargaff, "On Some of the Biological Consequences of Base-Pairing in Nucleic Acids" in *Developmental and Metabolic Control Mechanisms and Neoplasia* (Baltimore: Williams and Wilkins, 1965), p. 7.

8. O. T. Avery, C. M. MacLeod, M. McCarty, "Studies on the Chemical Nature of the Substance Inducing Transformation of Pneuomococcal Types" in *Journal of Experimental Medicine* (1944), 79, 137.

9. E. Chargaff, "Chemical Specificity of Nucleic Acids and Mechanism of their Enzymatic Degradation" in *Experientia* (1950), 6, 20.

10. J. D. Watson and F. H. C. Crick, "Molecular Structure of Nucleic Acids" in *Nature* (1953), 171, 737.

CHAPTER FOUR

Bitter Fruits from the Tree of Knowledge

1. John Donne, "An Anatomie of the World" *The First Anniversary*, lines 205–14.

2. Avery, MacLeod, McCarty, *op. cit.*

3. G. Wolstenholme (ed.), *Man and His Future* (Boston: Little, Brown, 1963).

4. E. Chargaff, *Essays on Nucleic Acids* (Amsterdam: Elsevier, 1963), p. 161.

5. A. Einstein, H. Born, and M. Born, *Briefwechsel 1916–1955* (Munich: Nymphenburger Verlagshandlung, 1969).

6. Simone Weil, *La pesanteur et la grâce* (Paris: Union Générale d'Editions, 1967), p. 133. Translation: "Science today must search for a source of inspiration higher than itself or it must perish. Science offers only three points of interest: (1) technical applications; (2) chess game; (3) the way toward God. (The chess game is embellished with competitions, prizes, and medals.)"

CHAPTER FIVE

Building the Tower of Babble

1. Watson, *The Double Helix*, p. 132.

2. Chargaff, *Essays in Nucleic Acids*.

3. Einstein, Born, Born, *op. cit.*

4. J. D. Watson and F. H. C. Crick, "Genetic Implications of the Structure of Deoxyribonucleic Acid" in *Nature* (1953), 171, 964. See also Watson and Crick, "Molecular Structure of Nucleic Acids."
5. *Ibid.*
6. Chargaff, "Chemical Specificity of Nucleic Acids and Mechanism of their Enzymatic Degradation."
7. Watson and Crick, *Ibid.*
8. Chargaff, "On Some of the Biological Consequences of Base-Pairing in the Nucleic Acids."

CHAPTER SIX
Profitable Wonders

1. Avery, MacLeod, McCarty, *op. cit.*
2. Chargaff, "Chemical Specificity of Nucleic Acids and Mechanism of their Enzymatic Degradation."
3. Hegel, *Encyclopedia of the Philosophical Sciences,* paragraph 353, addendum.

CHAPTER SEVEN
Triviality in Science: A Brief Meditation on Fashions

1. H. Zuckerman and R. K. Merton, "Patterns of Evaluation in Science: Institutionalization, Structure and Functions of the Referee System" in *Minerva* (1971), 9, 66.
2. Chargaff, "On Some of the Biological Consequences of Base-Pairing in the Nucleic Acids."
3. R. Barthes, *Système de la mode* (Paris: Le Seuil, 1967).

CHAPTER EIGHT
Voices in the Labyrinth:
Dialogues Around the Study of Nature

1. Translation: ". . . and you rest in yourself, while we are flung about in tribulations."
2. This is from the inscription over the gate of hell in Dante's *Inferno,* Canto III, line 7: "No things were made before me . . ."
3. Translation: ". . . For as you began, thus will you remain."
4. Translation: "The slightest motion matters to the whole of nature, the entire ocean is changed by one stone."

5. From Pascal's *Pensées,* Lafuma No. 553.

6. This is from Tertullianus *Apologeticus,* 50, 13. Translation: "The seed is the blood of the Christians."

7. Translation: "Blood is the seed of the sciences."

8. From William Dunbar's "Lament for the Makaris," lines 5–8; *pleasance* = delight, *brunkle* = brittle, *sle* = wily, *Timor mortis conturbat me* = the fear of death confounds me.

9. From Pope's "Epistle to Dr. Arbuthnot," line 310.

10. From Bacon's *Novum Organon,* Aphor. CXXIX.

11. The reference is to La Rochefoucauld's *Maximes,* no. 26.

12. L. Wittgenstein, *Über Gewissheit* (Frankfurt: Suhrkamp, 1970), no. 106, p. 36.

13. *Ibid.,* no. 286, p. 76.

14. Translation by Dryden:
    > Before the passage, horrid Hydra stands,
    > And Briareus with all his hundred hands;
    > Gorgons, Geryon with his triple frame;
    > And vain Chimaera vomits empty flame.

15. From *Report of the Foreign Secretary, National Academy of Sciences,* April 1973, p. 36.

Acknowledgments

I should like to thank the Trustees of Columbia University (Chapter One), The American Association for the Advancement of Science (Chapters Two and Three), Birkhäuser Verlag (Chapter Three), Chicago University Press (Chapters Four, Seven, and Eight), Macmillan Journals Ltd. (Chapter Five), the New York Academy of Sciences (Chapter Six), and Elsevier Scientific Publishing Co. (first section of Chapter Eight) for permission to reprint. I also want to express my warmest thanks to Miss Elsa Hayn for her help with the manuscript.

Erwin Chargaff

About the Author

Dr. Erwin Chargaff was born in Austria (1905) and educated at the University of Vienna where he studied chemistry, literary history, and philosophy. After receiving the Ph. D. degree in 1928 he continued his education at Yale University, the University of Berlin, and the Institut Pasteur in Paris. Since 1935 he has belonged to the faculty of Columbia University where he is now Professor Emeritus and former chairman of the Department of Biochemistry of the College of Physicians and Surgeons.

He is the holder of honorary doctorates from Columbia University and the University of Basel and the recipient of several important prizes, among others from the French and Dutch Academies of Sciences. Other awards include the National Medal of Science and the Gregor Mendel Medal. He is a member of the National Academy of Sciences, the American Academy of Arts and Sciences, the Royal Physiographic Society of Sweden, and of the German Academy of Naturalists Leopoldina.

In his research work he has ranged widely through many fields of chemistry and biochemistry. His foremost contribution has, perhaps, consisted in laying the groundwork for our present understanding of the nucleic acids and their role in genetics.

He has published more than 300 scientific papers, mostly in English, but also in German and French, in addition to literary texts in German. He is a frequent contributor to such general periodicals as *Perspectives in Biology and Medicine* (Chicago) and *Scheidewege* (Stuttgart), the editor of a fundamental treatise *The Nucleic Acids* in 3 volumes (New York and London), and the author of *Essays on Nucleic Acids* (Amsterdam).

About the Editor of This Series

Ruth Nanda Anshen, philosopher and editor, plans and edits *World Perspectives, Religious Perspectives, Credo Perspectives, Perspectives in Humanism, The Science of Culture* series, and *The Tree of Life* series. She also writes and lectures on the relationship of knowledge to the nature and meaning of man and his existence. She is the author of *The Reality of the Devil: Evil in Man,* a study of the phenomenology of evil.